15

AMAZING & INSPIRING STORIES

ON HOW THE WORLD'S GREATEST ATHLETES BECAME LEGENDS

IN BASEBALL, FOOTBALL, HOCKEY, BASKETBALL, SOCCER, TENNIS, GOLF & MORE

TERRENCE ARMSTRONG

CONTENTS

INTRODUCTION

Becoming a legend isn't an easy task. You need more than pure skill, it's about showing that you're close to perfection, saving your team or individual game repeatedly from the jaws of defeat, and illustrating that you are better than the best of the best. However, it's also about having the right character and mental attitude. It's often this that lifts a talented player to the ranks of legend.

Players don't choose to become legends, it is something that the fans bestow on them. But they usually have a fantastic story to tell and lessons that you can learn. In this book, we're going to take a look at 15 of the world's greatest athletes who became legends.

BABE RUTH
BASEBALL

Babe Ruth was born in 1895 in Baltimore, Maryland, and would go on to become perhaps the biggest legend that the world of baseball has ever known. His birth name was George Herman Ruth. He has gone down in history as the man who changed baseball forever.

Prior to Babe Ruth, baseball focused on strategy and maintaining maximum speed to get the players between bases. Ruth adopted a different approach. He hit the ball with such power and precision that he could drive it right out of the field and into the stadium. Babe Ruth didn't invent the home run. However, he did make people realize that it could be an integral part of any game. The ability to successfully hit multiple home runs is one of the reasons Ruth became known as a legend to fans and teammates alike.

Ruth's career started out as fairly normal. He had a difficult childhood and was sent to St. Mary's Industrial School for Boys when he was just seven years old. The school was an orphanage and a reformatory. It was here that he was first introduced to baseball and the school's prefect of discipline encouraged him. Interestingly, despite being left-handed, he was forced to wear mitts and gloves designed for right-handed players. The skills that he learned there earned him a spot with the minor-league Baltimore Orioles. It was an international League team owned and managed by Jack Dunn. There is little information about how this occurred but what is true is that Ruth worked for Dunn for just 30 minutes and was signed. He had to travel to North Carolina for training and was the subject of many pranks by his older teammates. It's at this time, he earned the nickname "Babe." It's not known exactly why he was given the nickname, but it was a fairly common one at that time.

His first professional appearance was in early March 1914. Ruth played shortstop and pitched the last two innings. When batting, he managed to hit a home run into the right field. The local news reported that the ball traveled further than it did than when the already legendary Jim Thorpe hit a home run on the same field. He went onto pitch for the Orioles in their next game and, after a slow start, he managed to pitch a scoreless fifth and sixth innings. He quickly became established as a star pitcher with a certain amount of skill when on the plate. When the new Federal League started, the Baltimore Terrapins managed to gain a place in the Federal League, giving Baltimore a team in the major league for the first time in many years. Ruth was still with the Orioles who were largely unheard of. But, the boost for the Terrapins drew attention to the Orioles. Unfortunately, they were struggling both on the field and financially. The owner chose to sell his best players and managed to get Ruth a position with the Boston Red Sox who played in the American League.

Despite winning his first game as a pitcher with the Red Sox, he was rarely used by them, even after he finally convinced them to let him play two exhibition matches and won both. He was even sent to a minor league team. Over the following two years, he sporadically pitched for the Red Sox and hit an impressive home run off a ball from Jack Warhop when playing against the New York Yankees. His pitching was good enough to win a starting spot but the Red Sox already had a good team of pitchers, which limited the number of appearances that he made. Ruth did manage to gain a good reputation as a pitcher. However, his frequent home runs were attracting attention.

Ruth's 1916 season was excellent and he managed a 23-12 with a 1.75 ERA for the season, helping the Red Sox win the World Series. Unfortunately, life wasn't as kind to him and after an outburst on the field, he rarely saw play. However, it was America's entry into WWI and the loss of some of the best players that gave Ruth his break. Although he was considered the best left-handed pitcher in the game, he was tired of playing one out of four or five games. The Red Sox had a temporary manager with little experience and he was heavily influenced by the players. They had noticed the crowd was larger when Ruth batted and convinced the manager to play Ruth as a batter when he wasn't pitching.

Ruth stepped up and hit 11 home runs in the war-shortened 1918 season. It gave him the joint most home runs in the league with Tilly Walker. Ruth was a great pitcher. His skill at throwing the ball took the Red Sox to the World Series in 1918. It was the third and last World Series victory for him as a pitcher. Next season saw the Red Sox perform badly and, knowing they weren't in the running for the Series, Ruth was allowed to bat during games. He drew in the crowds and in 1919, hit an amazing 29 home runs, taking the league record.

It was the start of his legend. That year, he was sold to the New York Yankees who took him as a batter. In 1920, he hit 54 home runs and in 1921, he managed 59 home runs. It was these feats that ensured he was known to everyone in the country, not just sporting fans.

In the postwar years, Ruth became America's symbol. His size and power, combined with very human flaws, emphasized everything that America had to offer and this helped him become a legend.

FUN FACTS ABOUT BABE RUTH

1. During his life Ruth donated a significant amount of money to various charities.
2. He always wore Jersey number 3.
3. He was fast and stole home 10 times in his career.
4. Babe Ruth thought he was born February 7, 1894, but discovered in 1934 that he was actually born February 6, 1895!
5. His record of 714 home runs remains unbeaten.

QUICK TRIVIA TEST

When was Babe Ruth born?

1895

Where did he spend most of his childhood?

St. Mary's Industrial School for Boys

Who did he play for as a pitcher?

Boston Red Sox

When was he sold to the Yankees?

1919

How many home runs did he score in 1921?

59

FIVE LIFE LESSONS

1. It's always possible to turn your life around

Babe Ruth was known for constantly getting into trouble, especially when he was young. It's believed this is why he was sent to the orphanage and reformatory school. However, this turned out to be good for him because he found baseball and adapted his lifestyle. It may not have changed his attitude completely but it helped a lot. It shows that you can always turn your life around, you just need the right catalyst.

2. Never give up!

Ruth was one of the best pitchers in the game but he wanted to be more than that. Despite frequently requesting to bat, he was frequently refused the opportunity. However, he never gave up and finally got a chance when the season was going poorly for the team. That changed everything and effectively created the legend, because he never gave up.

3. Give it your all

Regardless of what you are doing, you should always give it your all. Babe Ruth once said "I always swing at the ball with all my light. I hit or miss big." It's a good approach to have in life, always put in maximum effort, even if it doesn't always work out as expected.

4. You can't always win

Babe Ruth is known as an amazing pitcher and an even better batter. However, even the greatest can win every game and every tournament, especially when playing a team game. Accept that you can't always win and learn from the failures. It will make you a better player and person.

5. Seize any opportunity

You never know when your opportunity will come. If it wasn't for the war, Babe Ruth may have been the greatest batter the world never knew. Fortunately for him, the war forced baseball teams to change their teams and their playing staff, which gave Ruth the opportunity to show his real skills.

JOE MONTANA
AMERICAN FOOTBALL

Joseph Clifford Montana Jr. was born on June 11, 1956, in Pennsylvania. From a young age, Montana showed he was interested in sports, allowing his father to teach him the basics of the game. He joined his first youth football team when he was just eight years old. Interestingly, the minimum age was nine, so his father changed the year of his birth to allow him to play. Although he was fascinated by football, the young Montana also played baseball and basketball. His father even started a local basketball team so that Montanan could play more. Impressively, North Carolina State even offered him a basketball scholarship. That's how good he was!

For his first two years at high school, Montana was simply a backup for the football team. It was only as a junior that he earned a place as a starting quarterback. This was when the team started to see how skilled he was. Montana remained the starting quarterback for the rest of his time at High School. His performances were watched by colleges and after a particularly good outing against Monessen High School, he was offered a football scholarship by Notre Dame. In his first year, he wasn't allowed to play for the varsity team due to college rules. However, Montana was given several opportunities by the coach to shine in his sophomore year, and seized every one of them. Of particular note was his participation in the defeat of North Carolina, who had been leading 14-6. Montana started when there was just one minute and two seconds left of play.

Amazingly, in that short period, he had 129 passing yards, effectively securing a 21-14 win for Notre Dame.

He repeated the result in the next game. Montana came on in the last quarter with Notre Dame down 10-30 against the Air Force. By the time the game finished, Notre Dame had come back to win 31-30. An injury put him out of action for the 1976 season. In 1977, he showed the same ability again, coming on for Notre Dame with 11 minutes left while they were 14-24 down. The game finished with Notre Dame winning 31-24. He was finally made the starting quarterback.

In 1978, Montana was responsible for another comeback by Notre Dame against the Pitt Panthers and nearly achieved the same feat against the Fighting Irish. However, it was his performance in the Cotton Bowl in January 1979 that showed everyone how great he was. It's one of his most celebrated games. Notre Dame played Houston and Montana was fighting off hypothermia throughout the second quarter. He was given intravenous fluids and chicken soup to warm him up. He returned to the field late in the third quarter when Houston was leading 34-12. Montana leaped into action, ensuring three touchdowns in the dying eight minutes of the game, giving Notre Dame the win 35-34! It's fondly remembered as the chicken soup game.

Joe Montana was selected in the 1979 NFL draft by the San Francisco 49ers. As fourth quarterback, he saw little action in the 1979–1980 season. However, when he became the starting quarterback for the 1981 season, the 49ers saw a change in luck. They finished the regular season with 13 wins and 3 losses. Two of the games were won via Montana's trademark fourth-quarter comeback. This was the first of many with the club. In fact, in his time with the club, Montana helped the 49ers win 26 games via a fourth-quarter comeback. It was this ability to perform under immense pressure that earned him the nickname "Mr. Cool."

The following years are littered with incidents regarding Montana's impressive play, especially when the team was under immense pressure. By 1989, Montana had been to the Super Bowl three times. However, Montana is said to have been particularly gratified by the 1989 trip because the process of getting there had been much harder than in previous visits. This fact must have inspired Montana because he gave one of the best performances of his career, completing 23 of 36 passes and creating a Super Bowl record of 357 yards and two touchdowns. Despite an impressive performance, their opponents, the Cincinnati Bengals were winning 16-13 with only 3:20 left in the game. Montana again picked up the slack. In that short space of time, he completed 8 out of 9 passes for 92 yards and then threw the game-winning touchdown via a pass to John Taylor. There were just 34 seconds left when they won. It's worth noting that he took them back to the Super Bowl and another victory (his fourth) in 1990.

Montana was unfortunately injured and out of action for two years, ultimately prompting a trade from the 49ers to the Kansas City Chiefs. While there were no more Super Bowls for Montana, he helped the Chiefs achieve their best playing record and inspired the team and the fans. However, it was the fans that really impressed Montana. There are so many and they are so loyal and, as Montana said, when they sing the National Anthem and then say the "Home of the Chiefs," your hair will stand up on end, every time.

Joe Montana was inducted into the NFL Pro Football Hall of Fame in 2000. He had 31 fourth-quarter comeback victories and 10 playoff appearances in 11 full seasons. That's a record that may never be broken.

FUN FACTS ABOUT JOE MONTANA

1. Joe Montana was born in a coal-mining town.
2. He's the only player to ever have two 95+ yard touchdown passes.
3. As a child, his favorite sport was basketball!
4. He has won four Super Bowls and has three Super Bowl MVP awards.
5. By the end of his career, he had over 40,000 passing yards.

QUICK TRIVIA TEST

What is Montana's full name?

Joseph Clifford Montana Jr

When was he born?

1956

Who offered him a basketball scholarship?

North Carolina State

Who played in the chicken soup game?

Notre Dame vs Huston. Notre Dame ended up winning 35-34

How many fourth-quarter comebacks did Montana instigate for the 49ers?

26, (he did it 31 times in his career)

FIVE LIFE LESSONS

1. Never quit!

Montana is known as Mr. Cool because he was so good under pressure. He was the ultimate example of never quitting under pressure. His record of 31 fourth-quarter comebacks shows why it's so good not to quit and to stay cool. After all, he's proof that you can still win no matter how late it is in the game.

2. Teamwork matters

Joe Montana is one of the greatest quarterbacks to ever play the game. However, as even he'll admit, he couldn't win the game by himself. Sure, he can throw the ball with incredible accuracy over large distances. But there has to be someone there to catch it. If you're part of a team, remember that every player is important.

3. Legends are born from consistently performing special deeds

Pure talent doesn't create a legend. You need to excel in those moments when others are ready to give up hope. If your actions can restore hope you should do everything in your power to do so. But, doing it once makes you a great player, doing it over and over again will make you a legend. In short, use your skills for the benefit of the team!

4. Imagine it to make it possible

Montana once said, "Winners, I am convinced, imagine their dreams first. They want it with all their heart and expect it to come true. There is, I believe, no other way to live."

If you adopt this mentality and prepare your mind before your body, you too can be a winner.

5. Give it your all

You can't win every time, that's simply an impossibility because there are so many variables beyond your control. But you can look at yourself and your performance afterward and be proud that you gave it your all. That's what counts, win or lose.

As Montana once said, "When the game is over I just want to look at myself in the mirror, win or lose, and know I gave it everything I had."

WAYNE GRETZKY
ICE HOCKEY

Even people who have never played or watched ice hockey have heard of Wayne Gretzky, fondly referred to as "the Great One." He's become a legend on and off the ice thanks to his efforts and achievements while playing.

Gretzky was born in January 1961 in Brantford, Ontario, Canada. He enjoyed a close-knit family life and this was an important part of him becoming "the Great One." His love of ice hockey started as a youngster. His father, Walter Gretzky, was a hockey fan and inspired Gretzky and his brothers to play from an early age. He's famous for having built an ice rink in his backyard, allowing the young Gretzky to practice and hone his skills for hours every day. It's not surprising that Wayne Gretzky also developed a love of the sport.

Of course, an early introduction is nothing without skill, and Gretzky had bucketloads of that. By the time he was five years old, he was running rings around kids much older than him. His talent was becoming obvious and Gretzky's family encouraged him to work hard and make the most of his abilities. It was advice that Gretzky took to heart.

Others started to take notice when he got a place on the Sault Ste. Marie Greyhounds in the Ontario Hockey League. He achieved an impressive 70 goals and 112 assists in one season, creating the first of many records. Gretzky was noted to have fantastic puck control. However, it was more than that. He seemed capable of reading the game and the players, allowing him to know where the play would be, steal the puck, and deliver astonishing passes.

It was impossible to ignore his talent and the Indianapolis Racers snapped him up in 1978, when he was just 17. While there, he played some incredible ice hockey. But what really sealed his status as a once-in-a-lifetime player and a legend was his time with the Edmonton Oilers, where he achieved 215 points in a single season. That's a record that has yet to be broken.

However, what Gretzky really brought with him was a transformation. Before he joined the NHL, games were consistently played by brute force. Every team sought to power their way through, obliterating the other side in the process. Injuries were extremely common. Gretzky changed the way that the game was played. His desire to win was so strong, and his skill so great, that he could bind any team together. Gretzky played with finesse, creating plays, identifying and blocking plays, and encouraging the team to work together. Impressively, this approach worked and the Oilers started to win games. It became obvious that brute force could be overcome with teamwork, creativity, and skill. This became the norm for the game, making every game more challenging and more exciting. His actions and impact have inspired a generation of young players, encouraging them to adopt his playing style and attitude. It's a testimony to "the Great One" that so many people have copied his approach.

Gretzky enjoyed a record-breaking career in the NHL. Many of his records are yet to be beaten and may never be seriously challenged. For example, Gretzky's career points total was 2,857. No one has come close to that number since. His 215 in one season was achieved in the 1985–1986 season. It has yet to be beaten but shows what is possible in the world of ice hockey.

Naturally, the Edmonton Oilers benefited from his skill. They won four Stanley Cups in the 1980s with Gretzky as he transformed and inspired the entire team. The team became the dominant force in the league, all thanks to the efforts of Gretzky. Of course, it was Gretzky's ability to find space and pass accurately that helped to ensure they became a force to be reckoned with.

However, there was a twist. In a surprise announcement, Gretzky was released from the Oilers in 1988 and transferred to the Los Angeles Kings. While it shocked the fans, it did miracles for the game. At the time, hockey was nowhere near as popular in the US as it was in Canada. The transfer made him even more of a legend.

Not only did Gretzky play amazing ice hockey in Los Angeles, he inspired the US, and the world. Suddenly, people everywhere wanted to play ice hockey. The sport became popular in an array of unusual places, effectively changing the trajectory and popularity of the game across the globe. It's understandable why Gretzky became a legend!

It's important to note that Gretzky worked as hard off the ice as on. While playing, he appeared to have an uncanny ability to see where the puck was going and anticipate virtually any play. His shooting and passing skills can best be described as a work of art. These are a result of practice and his ability to see the game and potential plays before they happened. Part of this is a skill he was born with, the other part he learned by watching and playing as many games as possible.

Many have compared him to a conductor with his team being the orchestra. He certainly had great leadership qualities and an impressive ability to make the players around him better. His calm and focused demeanor has made him an inspiration to young athletes across the globe, all of which hope to emulate him. What more can a legend do?

FUN FACTS ABOUT WAYNE GRETZKY

1. When Gretzky retired, every hockey team retired his number 9 jersey!
2. Gretzky coached the Canadian men's hockey team to an Olympic gold at the 2002 Winter Olympics.
3. When he played and scored at the age of six, he was playing against 10-year-olds.
4. Gretzky's sons, Trevor and Ty, are both pursuing careers in ice hockey.
5. His career spanned two decades, he retired in April 1999.

QUICK TRIVIA TEST

How old was he when he joined the Indianapolis Racers?

17

What was his career points total?

2,857

How many points did he score in the 1985–1986 season, setting a yet-to-be-beaten record in the process?

215

How many Stanly Cups did the Oilers win with Gretzky?

4

What did his dad build in the backyard for him?

An ice rink

FIVE LIFE LESSONS

1. Work hard

Gretzky's parents, particularly his father, taught him and encouraged him to practice hard and work hard at his game, no matter how much skill he appeared to have. It was this hard work and dedication that turned a talented player into a legend.

You have to be prepared to work hard if you want to succeed in anything.

2. Think of others

Gretzky holds the record for most points scored in a career. It's a record that will be difficult to beat. However, what his record doesn't show is how many times he gave the goal to others. Gretzky always remembered his teammates and knew where they were. It was this that helped the Oilers dominate ice hockey for such a long period.

3. Records aren't everything

When Wayne Gretzky retired, he had 61 NHL records. It shows just how impressive he was as a player. However, he is prouder of his influence on the game and the pleasure he had playing than the records.

Remember that if you excel at anything, records aren't everything, you need someone to share them with.

4. You can't always win but you can always try

Gretzky once said, "You miss one hundred percent of the shots you don't take." It's true that any shot left untaken is an opportunity to win that has passed you by. Whether you're playing ice hockey or dealing with life, you may not be able to always win, but you should always try your hardest.

5. Humility is important

Gretzky is "the Great One" because he achieved so much for ice hockey. However, he managed to stay humble throughout his career. He states this is due to his attitude. As he once said, "When you win, say nothing, when you lose, say less." This approach helps you to be humble and appreciative, which it turn makes you more likeable and a better player.

MICHAEL JORDAN
BASKETBALL

Michael Jordan is a much-loved figure and perhaps one of the best-known athletes in the world. It wasn't just his skill with a basketball that won him legendary status. He's also starred in *Space Jam* as himself and has spent years giving back to the sport, including purchasing a basketball team and becoming the first-ever former NBA player to become a majority owner of an NBA team.

Jordan was born in February 1963 in Brooklyn, New York. However, he was brought up in North Carolina and attended Laney High School. As a child, he idolized his older brother, Larry. Jordan frequently played basketball with his dad. It was this, and the love that he had for his athletic brother, that drove him to basketball. However, despite having talent, at 5'11" he was too short and too skinny to make the sophomore team. Fortunately, he had a growth spurt, reaching 6'3", and joined the varsity team in his junior years. Without that growth spurt, the world may never have seen the talents of Michael Jordan!

While he stayed mainly in the shadows for his first year at the University of Borth Carolina, he played, and shone, in the NCAA championship game against Georgetown. It was the first time of many that he thwarted a Patrick Ewing victory. He did it in style, taking the winning basket on a 16-foot jumper to win victory for his team 63-62. It naturally led him to the Chicago Bulls, third overall pick in the 1984 draft.

It wasn't as easy as it sounds. The assistant coach at UNC remembers Jordan telling him he wanted to be the best player UNC had ever seen and promised that he would work harder than every other player. He was true to his word, Jordan spent three years at UNC and gained a reputation for never stopping. Even his teammate James Worthy commented, "After about 2.5 hours of hard practice, I'm walking off the floor, like, drenched [in] sweat, tired. And, here comes Michael pushing me back on the floor, wanting to play a little one-on-one, wanting to see where his game was."

As good as his performance had been so far, it was merely a backdrop to what was to come. From the moment Jordan started playing for the Bulls, he was building his reputation. He's known as a scoring machine. However, the truth is, he was an impressive athlete. Not only could he sprint fast, his skill with the ball and acrobatic dunks meant he dazzled fans on nearly every appearance. He also impressed his team, which was his aim. As Jordan himself said, "From the first day of practice, my mentality was: 'Whoever is the team leader of the team, I'm going to be going after him. And I'm not going to do it with my voice.' Because I had no voice. I had no status. I had to do it with the way that I played." His approach worked on the fans and his teammates. Perhaps more importantly, he showed the team, the fans, and the world how hard he was prepared to work.

Jordan's efforts didn't go unrewarded. He played for the Chicago Bulls from 1984–1993, when he suddenly left after the murder of his father. Jordan spent two years playing minor league baseball before returning to the Bulls. He returned in 1993 and played with them until he retired again in 1999. His list of achievements during his 15 seasons on the court is impressive: 6 NBA championships with the Bulls, 5 NBA MVPs, 14 NBA All-Stars, 10 All-NBA First Team, and many more.

However, while his play and scoring ability was unrivaled, he earned the title of legend through his ability to deliver when the team needed it the most. It didn't matter whether the game was 5 minutes in or 30 seconds from the end, Jordan could elevate his game during those crucial moments. It earned him the nickname "Air Jordan" and he's recognized as one of the greatest clutch performers in history.

Jordan has delivered many stunning performances so it can be hard to define the best ones. However, it's worth mentioning his game-winning shot against the Jazz, which gave the Bulls their sixth NBA Championship title. The clock was definitely running out as the Bulls were losing by three points. Jordan stripped the ball from Malone in the defensive end, hurled himself across the court, and launched a shot from 20 foot out with just 5.2 seconds left. It bounced off the backboard and dropped straight through the net, giving the Bulls the game and Jordan a fitting end to his career with the Chicago Bulls.

Jordan also became a legend through his exploits off the court. He linked with many brands to create sponsorship deals. Perhaps his most famous was with Nike, allowing the iconic Air Jordan sneaker to be created. What was impressive is that this type of sponsorship is taken for granted today. At the time, it was revolutionary. In effect, Jordan changed the way that athletes were marketed.

Jordan is undoubtedly one of the best players ever seen on the court. His skill and the number of records he set are legendary. However, it's his calm demeanor, his constant drive to improve, and his sheer athletic ability that ensure this legend is unlikely to ever be beaten.

FUN FACTS ABOUT MICHAEL JORDAN

1. His net worth in 2020 was estimated to be $1.6 billion.
2. Michael Jordan starred in the film *Space Jam*.
3. If he hadn't been a basketball player, he was thinking of being a weatherman.
4. Jordan was inducted into the Naismith Memorial Basketball Hall of Fame in 2009.
5. Michael Jordan has five children and two of his sons play minor league basketball.

QUICK TRIVIA TEST

When was Michael Jordan born?

February 1963

In which year was he the third overall NBA draft pick?

1984

Why didn't he make the varsity team in his sophomore year?

He was too short at just 5'11"

Why did Jordan retire and start playing minor-league baseball?

Because his father had been murdered

How many NBA Championships did he win?

6

FIVE LIFE LESSONS

1. Never quit!

Michael Jordan once said, "I can accept failure, everyone fails at something. But I can't accept not trying." There were several times in his career when he could have chosen to give up. In fact, he may not even have started basketball if he didn't have his growth spurt, because he was considered too short.

Although it may have seemed like an insurmountable issue, he didn't give up. All you have to do is look at where his never-quit attitude got him and you can do the same!

2. Always give your all

Jordan was known for playing as hard in practice as he did in competitive games. His attitude was that you should always give it your all. As he said, "I don't do things half-heartedly. Because I know if I do, then I can expect half-hearted results."

It's a worthy sentiment and one that you should apply to your own life.

3. Look for your weaknesses

Everyone has weaknesses, it's part of life. However, instead of simply accepting the weaknesses, you can work on them and turn them into a strength. As Jordan once said, "My attitude is that if you push me towards something that you think is a weakness, then I will turn that perceived weakness into a strength."

This is a good attitude to adopt in life.

4. Never say never

Anything is possible and you should always be open to what possibilities are available to you. It may seem like you've finished something and will never do it again. However, as Michael Jordan once said, "One day, you might look up and see me playing the game at 50. Don't laugh. Never say never, because limits, like fears, are often just an illusion."

5. Don't forget that you're part of a team

No matter how great your talent is, in most sports and certainly in life, you're part of a bigger team. As Jordan said, "Talent wins games but teamwork and intelligence win championships." In other words, remember your team and use everyone's strengths and weaknesses to get the desired result.

I have included these free downloadable gifts to help light up your inner inspiration & reach your potential.

While you are reading through the stories, lessons and trivia, we recommend that you make use of all the bonuses we've attached here!

All our bonuses have been made specifically to help young athletes feel fired up, get inspired from the best to ever do it, and most importantly fall more in love with this incredible game!

Here's a list of what you're getting:

1) 250 Fun Facts From The World Of Sports
2) Sports Practice and Game Calendar
3) 5 Fun Exercise Drills for Kids
4) The BEST Advice From The Greatest Athletes Of All Time
5) The Mental Mindset Guided Meditation & Affirmation Collection
6) The Most Famous Events In Sports History And What They Can Teach Us

Now, it's over to you to scan the QR code, follow the instructions & get started!

LIONEL MESSI
SOCCER

Lionel Messi was born in June 1987 in Rosario, Santa Fe, Argentina. He was the third child. His father worked in a steel factory and his mother manufactured magnets. Messi spent much of his childhood kicking the ball around with his two older brothers. The whole family had a passion for the game. Interestingly, both of his older brothers also became professional soccer players.

By the time he was four years old, he was already playing for the local club, the Grandoli. His grandfather was the team coach. However, it was his maternal grandmother who really inspired him. She came to every one of his matches and training sessions. She died just before Messi turned 11 and it's believed that this is why he looks up and points to the sky when he scores—it's a tribute to his grandmother.

At the age of six, he joined the Newell's Old Boys club. He played for them for six years and scored close to 500 goals in that time. The youth side was known as nearly unbeatable. Messi's skills were becoming evident and he would regularly entertain the half-time crowd with ball tricks. However, a problem developed when Messi turned 11 and they discovered that he had a growth hormone deficiency and had effectively stopped growing. Despite his talents, the expectation in the industry was for soccer players to be physically big. Although some clubs showed an interest in him, his height stopped them from taking him on. His parent's health insurance only covered two years of treatment.

Fortunately, thanks to relatives in Catalonia, Barcelona reached out and offered him a contract, which included paying for his treatment.

The relocation to Barcelona was hard for Messi. At first, his family came with him. However, his mother, brothers, and little sister moved back to Argentina while he stayed with his father in Barcelona. He became homesick and was playing little soccer because as a foreigner, he could only play in friendlies and the Catalan League. Fortunately, he survived the year and was then enrolled in the Royal Spanish Football Federation, allowing him to play in all the matches and start forming friendships with his teammates. He went on to become an integral part of the Barcelona "Baby Dream Team," the greatest youth side to ever play for Barcelona. He scored 36 goals in 30 games in his first full season, a hint of what was to come.

At just 16 years, 4 months, and 23 days old, he debuted for the Barcelona first team. He came on as a substitute in the 75th minute. His first league goal as a senior didn't happen until May 2005, it made him the youngest-ever scorer for Barcelona. He was instrumental in the team winning the league title in the 2004–2005 season and again in the 2005–2006 season. The team also won the Champions League in 2006. By the 2008–2009 season, Messi was hitting his stride. He, alongside Samuel Eto'o and Thierry Henry, contributed to an impressive total of 100 goals across all competitions. At the time, it was a new record for the club. It was also the start of Messi setting records.

Messi has won the men's Ballon d'Or a staggering eight times. He's also won FIFA World Player of the Year seven times and La Liga Player of the Year nine times. Alongside this, he has six European Golden Shoes, two Laureus World Sports Awards, two World Cup Golden Balls, two UEFA Men's Player of the Year, and two Copa America Most Valuable Player.

Of course, these are simply accolades. What really makes Messi a legend is his ability to score goals. In a 20-year career, he has scored over 800 goals, many of which have been impressive. For example, in 2007, he played in the Copa Del Ray semi-final 1st leg, while he was still relatively unknown, and he scored a goal that reminded everyone of Diego Maradona, the Argentinian legend. Messi scooped up the ball in his half of the field and moved across the field in a methodical and determined fashion. He wound his way around no less than four Getafe defenders with precision dribbling and control. He then finished, by slipping around the goalkeeper and lofting the ball over a final defender trying to slide across the goal. It was both amazing and unbelievable, effectively illustrating his talent and how many of his future goals would be made.

Another of his impressive goals was in the 2015 Copa Del Rey final. In this instance, he received the ball from teammate Dani Alves and was immediately under attack by three Athletic players. Despite this, he displayed his precision ball control and practically danced around all three, glided around another one-on-one challenge, and slid the ball into the net, near the post as so many of his precision shots have been. It's unlikely any other player could have managed this feat.

Messi isn't just amazing on the field, scoring goal after goal, particularly when it seems like an impossible challenge; his skills have also made him a legend. But it's his effect on soccer that has cemented that legend. Since his unique display of ball control and precision dribbling, youth development and coaches across the world have increased focus on technical skills and ball control. It's fair to say that he's revolutionized the game and the way it's played.

FUN FACTS ABOUT LIONEL MESSI

1. Messi's full name is Luis Lionel Andres Messi.
2. In 2012, Messi scored 91 goals in one season, it's a record that has yet to be beaten.
3. Messi was given the number 10 jersey when Ronaldinho left Barcelona.
4. He is a citizen of Argentina, Italy, and Spain.
5. Messi has scored 50 goals in his career from direct free-kicks.

QUICK TRIVIA TEST

When was Messi born?

1987

Why does he point his finger to the sky when he scores?

As a tribute to his grandmother

Why were teams reluctant to take on the young player?

Because of his height and growth hormone deficiency

Which club gave Messi a chance to continue his soccer career when others were turning him down for his height?

Barcelona

How many goals did he score while with the Newell's Old Boys Club?

Nearly 500

FIVE LIFE LESSONS

1. Never quit!

Messi could have given up when he was told he had a growth hormone deficiency and teams were suddenly much less interested in him. That's despite the skills he had already displayed. He didn't give up and found a way (with the help of his parents) to become a legendary soccer player.

As Messi says, "You have to fight to reach your dream. You have to sacrifice and work hard for it."

2. Always work to be better

Messi is a legend, he has a natural talent that has been honed with hard work. However, that doesn't mean he's sitting pretty. The reason why he's still in demand and still playing impressive soccer in his mid-30s is that he is constantly striving to be better. That's something everyone should try to do.

As Messi says, "My ambition is always to get better and better."

3. Size doesn't matter

Despite treatment, Messi is still a small player. That doesn't stop him from being a great player, proving that size really doesn't matter. Remember that, whether you're big, small, or average size.

4. Follow your instincts

Many players swear by visualizing the game and believing that what they visualize can come true. Messi takes a different approach, relying on his instinct. As he says, "I never think about the play or visualize anything. I do what comes to me at that moment. Instinct. It has always been that way."

You can visualize or trust your instincts and it's essential to do what you think is best for you.

5. Think of others

Messi is more than a great soccer player. He is also a humanitarian who donates to charities and gives his time to help others. The more successful you are, the more important it is that you give back to your sport and the wider world.

As Messi says, "For my part, I try to do my bit to make people's lives more bearable, in particular children across the globe who are having problems."

ROGER FEDERER
TENNIS

Roger Federer was born on August 8, 1981, in Basel, Switzerland. He would go on to be one of the greatest tennis players of all time. Along the way, he would be ranked number one in the world at the end of the year on five separate occasions, be ranked number one for an impressive 310 weeks (approximately six years), and set a record as being the number one player in the world for 237 consecutive weeks. If that wasn't enough, he won 103 singles titles, the second most titles won by an individual, and 20 major men's titles. This includes a record-setting 8 Wimbledon titles!

It all started when he and his sister used to accompany his parents to the tennis courts. His parents worked for Ciba-Geigy Pharmaceuticals and were allowed to use the private courts on the company grounds. Federer started playing tennis when he was just three years old. By six, he had enrolled in tennis school and was quickly recognized as the best in his age group. Just two years later, his parents enrolled him in the elite junior program at the Old Boys Tennis Club, allowing Federer to compete against better players. It was here that Federer started to play his one-handed backhand. It's rumored he did so because his childhood idols, Boris Becker, Stefan Edberg, and Pete Sampras, all did the same. Thanks to his natural talent, he received individual and group training. It was at this school that he was first taught by Peter Carter, a former professional tennis player.

In 1993, he won the Swiss U12 National Junior Championships. This prompted him to give up the various other sports he was playing and focus solely on tennis. It worked as just two years later, he won the U14 Swiss national junior championship and was offered a place at the prestigious National Tennis Centre ibn Ecublens. Here, he studied and got to play tennis for three hours every day. However, it was initially a dark period in his life. The young Federer was the youngest at the academy and the main language spoken there was French. Federer came from a German-speaking part of Switzerland and didn't know French. Alongside feeling homesick, he was mildly bullied and was often on the verge of heading home.

Instead, he started playing and winning tournaments. Most notably, he won his first Wimbledon title in 1998 while still a junior player. He even won the junior Wimbledon doubles title. Impressively, the only junior circuit final he lost was the US Open Junior to David Nalbandian. Shortly afterward, he defeated Nalbandian in the semi-finals of the Junior Orange Bowl and went on to win the title and become the ITF Junior Champion while being ranked junior number one in the world.

However, it wasn't all plain sailing. At 17, in his first professional year, he finished the year ranking 301 in the world. His second year was better. His first title win was on the Challenger tour. He won the doubles final with Sander Groen on his 18th birthday! He also entered Wimbledon and the French Open, although lost both in the first round. However, it was enough to move him into the top 100 players in the world. By the end of 1999, he was ranked 64 in the world. By the end of 2000, with several singles victories under his belt, Federer had reached 29 in the world. But it was 2001 that really put him on the map.

At Wimbledon 2001, he played against Pete Sampras in the fourth round. Sampras was the number one seed but Federer beat him in five sets, breaking Sampras's winning streak of 31 Wimbledon games. However, he lost in the quarter-finals to Tim Henman.

Sadly, he lost his long-time coach and mentor, Peter Carter, to a car crash in 2002. This was the catalyst that elevated his game. After a few bad matches, Federer pulled himself together and played with more determination than ever. By the end of 2002, he was ranked 6 in the world.

While 2003 was a good year, 2004 was when he established his real dominance. This was the year he won three Grand Slam titles, the first person to ever achieve such a feat in one season. It elevated him to number one in the world. By the end of the year, he had won 11 singles titles, more than any other player in the last two decades. Impressively, he achieved another 11 singles victories in 2005 with a staggering 81 match victories and the third-best winning percentage (81-4 [95.2%]) of all time.

Unbelievably, he beat his own record in 2006, winning 12 singles titles and an impressive 92 wins, with just 5 losses. Federer also reached all four Grand Slam finals, the first person to do so since 1969. He won three of the four titles. It's a feat he repeated the following year.

Federer continued his success and dominance on the court. One of his most famous matches was at Wimbledon in 2007 when he played Nadal. It was a thrilling five-set match that many people have said was the greatest Wimbledon final ever. He won another three Grand Slam titles, becoming the only player to win three Grand Slams in three consecutive years. It also marked three years of being ranked the world number one continually.

The long list of wins leaves little doubt regarding Federer's skill with a racket. However, it's his humility off the court that encourages people to like and respect him. He's also known as a philanthropist. Federer has created his own foundation and has been involved in an array of charitable events. His attempts to give something back and the number of titles he has won are the reasons he's able to inspire thousands of people across the globe.

FUN FACTS ABOUT ROGER FEDERER

1. Federer has two citizenships: Swiss and South African.
2. He's played tennis in 23 different countries.
3. Federer's favorite food is Italian.
4. He was paid $15 million by Rolex for their ad deal.
5. When not playing tennis, Federer is a keen hiker.

QUICK TRIVIA TEST

When was Federer born?

August 8, 1981

Who were his childhood idols?

Boris Becker, Stefan Edberg, and Pete Sampras

What year did he first win Wimbledon?

1998 – as a junior player

What year did he first become world number one?

2004

How many Wimbledon titles did Federer get?

8

FIVE LIFE LESSONS

1. Adversity makes you stronger

When Federer's longtime mentor and coach died in a tragic car accident, he was devastated. It showed in his tennis as he failed to win any games. However, he turned himself around and drove forward with a new sense of determination, dedicating his wins to the memory of his coach.

This was a breakthrough point and shows that adversity can make you stronger. Just take the time to work through the issue first.

2. Be consistent

Winning every time is hard. Federer stayed number one in the world for many years. While skill plays a part in his success, he credits his wins with something more simple—consistency.

His play is consistent and he strives to keep it that way. Focusing on that reduces the pressure of playing and helps him maintain the right level in all his games. It's worth being consistent in all walks of life.

3. Believe in yourself

Federer once said, "It is always in my mind still that I can crush anybody. That's not an issue. But I think that is the same for most athletes. If you don't believe you can win tournaments anymore, then you can't do it."

It's valuable advice, if you want to consistently win, you need to believe in yourself.

4. Do it for yourself

You can do anything but you'll find it easier to be successful if you're doing it for yourself. It means you'll believe in your goal and even enjoy the activity. As Federer once said, "I'm not playing to prove anything to journalists. I'm playing for myself, for my fans, to make people happy."

5. Seize any opportunity

You never know when you'll get another opportunity the same or as good as the one in front of you. Instead of worrying about it or living to regret it, seize every opportunity and make the most of it. As Federer says, "I definitely need to use my chances when they come because definitely there won't be many."

TIGER WOODS
GOLF

Mention golf and most people will instantly think of Tiger Woods. It's not surprising, he has dominated the sport for years. True, he's won a record-setting 82 PGA Tours, but there is more to this legend than meets the eye.

Eldrick Tont Woods was born in December 1975 and is today recognized as one of the greatest golfers ever. He is perhaps one of the most famous living athletes and has been inducted into the World Golf Hall of Fame.

Woods is the only child of Kultida and Earl Woods. However, he does have a half-sister and two half-brothers. He gained the nickname Tiger as a child from his parents. It was, in part, due to his indomitable spirit and partly due to his father's friend, a South Vietnamese Colonel, who was often referred to as Tiger.

Wood's father was a keen athlete and introduced Woods to golf before he was two years old! Although clearly talented at golf, Woods initially wanted to play baseball like his father. Unfortunately, the young Woods tore his rotator cuff and decided baseball was no longer for him.

His skill at golf was already evident. In 1978, when he was just three, he played against comedian Bob Hope for *The Mike Douglas Show*. They played at the Navy course and Woods hit a 48 over nine holes. He hadn't even turned seven when he won the under-ten section of the Drive, Pitch, and Putt competition. When he was eight, he won the Junior World Golf Championships. He was allowed to play in the 9–10-year-old group, the youngest level available.

His first major national junior tournament was when he was 13 years old. Woods was paired with John Daly. Woods lost the game by just one stroke after Daly birdied three of the last four holes.

In 1990, at just 15 years old, Woods won the U.S. Junior Amateur Champion. He was the youngest person to ever win this and his record stood until 2010 when Jim Liu beat it. He won the U.S. Junior Amateur Champion in 1991 and 1992, becoming the only player to ever win this trophy three times.

At this stage, he naturally had a selection of golf scholarships offered by colleges. Woods chose Stanford University. While studying economics, he played in his first PGA Tour major—the 1995 Masters. He was the only amateur allowed to play. By the end of the tournament, he was ranked 41st.

The following year, aged 20, he turned professional and was immediately offered lucrative endorsement deals from Nike, Inc, and Titleist. He won his first major, the Masters, in April 1997 and instantly became the youngest ever winner of the tournament. Just two months later, he was officially number one in the World Golf Ranking, the fastest ascent to the top spot ever.

While Woods was still finding his feet in 1998; the 1999 season proved to be impressive. This was the year he had laser eye surgery and started a winning streak. By the end of the 1998 season, he had won eight tournaments, something not seen since Johnny Miller did the same in 1974.

Woods won six consecutive events on the PGA Tour, something that had not been seen since 1948! During this period, he won the U.S. Open and broke or tied nine tournament records in the process. It is often described as the greatest performance in golf history. He earned $800,000 from the tournament and set a record for winning by 15 strokes.

2001 was the year of the Tiger Slam. This was when he won the Masters and clinched four consecutive major professional golf titles, something that no one else has managed to do. His 2002 season was just as good as 2001. However, 2003 and 2004 were not good for him. Because Woods maintains his privacy, the exact reasons for this slump are unknown. It may have been because his father was extremely ill with cancer at this time. It could also be that he continued to play with Nike clubs even though the Titleist brand is far better suited to his style of play.

Fortunately, the old Tiger appeared the following year. In 2005 he regained the top spot in world rankings and won another six PGA Tour events. While 2006 was a rough year as his father died, Woods took some time off and then rebounded again, racking up 54 wins including 12 majors and breaking tour records for total majors won and total wins.

In 2008, Woods needed surgery on a badly injured knee. He announced his break from golf after beating Rocco Mediate in an 18-hole playoff. As everyone noted afterward, Woods was effectively playing on one leg and still beat everyone. The following years were rough, but in 2013, Woods was back in world-beating form. Since then he has continued to play well but has been hampered by an array of injuries. He still managed to win his 80th Tour-Championship in 2018, followed by the Masters in 2019. It also made him the second-oldest golfer to ever win the tournament.

Woods isn't just an amazing golfer. His presence in the sport has meant more people watch and follow the sport than ever before. He's raised the profile of the game and encouraged a lot of people to try it. But, through everything, Woods has remained humble and approachable. This has proved to be as important as his undoubtable skill in making him a legend.

FUN FACTS ABOUT TIGER WOODS

1. Wood stuttered as a child and overcame it via a two-year class.
2. Woods has severe myopia, which is why he's had laser eye surgery twice.
3. Woods is a Buddhist.
4. Woods has been ranked Golf number one in the world for a total of 683 weeks in his career.
5. He created the Tiger Woods Foundation to provide educational resources and opportunities to youth.

QUICK TRIVIA TEST

How many PGA Tours has he won?

82

What is Wood's real name?

Eldrick Tont Woods

How old was Woods when he went professional?

20

How many siblings does Woods have?

Two half-brothers and one half-sister

When did he play in his first major tournament?

When he was 13

FIVE LIFE LESSONS

1. You can overcome anything

Woods isn't known for having a stutter. In fact, it wasn't public knowledge until he wrote a letter to a young lad contemplating suicide. In it, he wrote "I know what it's like to be different and to sometimes not fit in. I also stuttered as a child and I would talk to my dog and he would sit there and listen until he fell asleep. I also took a class for two years to help me, and I finally learned to stop."

This was the first the world had heard of his stutter and his efforts to overcome it. Woods only disclosed it to help someone else. It shows you can overcome anything.

2. Be consistent

It can be hard to be consistent when there are so many outside pressures which can distract you. Woods has suffered the death of his father, an array of injuries, and a very public fallout from his affair.

Each of these events has affected his ability to play at the peak of his game. That's why, to maintain your form in all walks of life, you need to learn to put concerns aside and focus on delivering consistent performance. Being mentally prepared can help with this.

3. Keep trying!

Woods exploded onto the golf scene and instantly showed he was an impressive golfer. But even he can't win everything and acknowledges that there is always room for improvement. In short, keep trying to get better, it will help you succeed.

As Woods said, "No matter how good you get you can always get better, and that's the exciting part."

4. Failing sometimes is good

Woods once said, "It's okay to fail. Failing does not shape your personality; it's how you react upon your failure. Do you dust yourself off and mope or do you dust yourself off and come back stronger the next time? Eventually you will win."

In short, you can learn from your failings and become a better player, that's what makes failing an important part of winning.

5. Always work on developing your skills

Woods once said, "Talent is something you are born with, and a skill is something you develop. 99% of what you need to succeed in golf are skills."

Woods is naturally talented, but his skills have come from years of practice. It's never too soon to start practicing.

I have included these free downloadable gifts to help light up your inner inspiration & reach your potential.

While you are reading through the stories, lessons and trivia, we recommend that you make use of all the bonuses we've attached here!

All our bonuses have been made specifically to help young athletes feel fired up, get inspired from the best to ever do it, and most importantly fall more in love with this incredible game!

Here's a list of what you're getting:

1) 250 Fun Facts From The World Of Sports
2) Sports Practice and Game Calendar
3) 5 Fun Exercise Drills for Kids
4) The BEST Advice From The Greatest Athletes Of All Time
5) The Mental Mindset Guided Meditation & Affirmation Collection
6) The Most Famous Events In Sports History And What They Can Teach Us

Now, it's over to you to scan the QR code, follow the instructions & get started!

MUHAMMAD ALI
BOXING

Most people will agree that Muhammad Ali is the greatest heavyweight boxer that ever lived. His performance in the ring is certainly enough to earn him legendary status. However, for Ali, it was more than just the sport. He is often regarded as one of the most significant sports stars of the 20th century. His impact reaches beyond the world of sports.

Ali was born in Louisville, Kentucky, on January 17, 1942. His birth name was Cassius Marcellus Clay Jr. Both his parents worked, his father as a sign and billboard painter, while his mother was a domestic helper. Ali attended the local Central High School in Louisville but suffered from dyslexia. This condition affected his ability to read and write at school and throughout life.

It's important to remember that when Ali was a child, racial segregation was the norm. His mother recalls him being denied a glass of water in a store because of his skin color. This affected his outlook, as did the 1955 murder of Emmett Till.

Ali's path to boxing is unusual. As a 12-year-old, he had his bicycle stolen. He was fuming and told the police officer Joe E. Martin that he was going to whup the thief. The police office was also a boxing coach and advised the young Ali to learn how to box first. At first, the young Ali wasn't interested, but then he saw amateur boxers on the television and decided to give it a go.

Ali trained hard and entered his first professional bout in 1954 against a local amateur. He won via a split decision and it was the start of an impressive amateur career. In total, Ali had 100 wins and 5 losses as an amateur.

In October 1960, Ali had his first professional fight. He won via a six-round decision against Tunney Hunsaker. In the following three years, Ali managed 19 wins and zero losses. An impressive 15 of the wins were by knockout. He beat some of the biggest names in the sport, such as George Logan, Tony Esperti, and Henry Cooper. That's not to say the fights were easy! When fighting Cooper, Ali was floored by a good left hook right at the end of the fourth round. He was saved by the bell, allowing him to recover and win the fight in the fifth round, thanks in part to Cooper's seriously cut eye.

However, his fight with Doug Jones may have been even tougher. Jones was the number two, Ali was the number three heavyweight contender. Jones staggered Ali in the first round. However, by the end of the fight, Ali won unanimously. The result was greeted with boos and debris was thrown into the ring as they were on Jones' home turf.

It was during this period that Ali became known as a big mouth and a bragger. It was a conscious decision on his part because one of his heroes, Gorgeous George the wrestler, had advised him that trash talk was a great way to attract the crowds.

His wins led him to a fight against Sonny Liston. The date was set for February 1964. Liston had a serious reputation. His personality was intimidating, he was a dominating fighter, and he had ties to the mob along with a criminal past. Although he won both, Ali hadn't performed well against Cooper or Jones, making the odds 8:1 underdog. Liston had just destroyed the heavyweight champion Floyd Patterson.

Ali took every opportunity possible to have a go at Liston, calling him the big ugly bear and similar insults. It was to ensure a massive crowd. The fight was epic. The moment the bell rang, Liston rushed at Ali, potentially looking to finish it quickly. Ali was far more nimble and used his speed to dance around Liston. Toward the end of the first round, Ali saw his chance and hit Liston repeatedly with jabs.

The second round saw a more focused Liston, but he was unable to make his mark. Then, at the beginning of round three, Ali hit Liston with a combination of punches that buckled his knees and gave him a cut under his left eye. Liston had never been cut before but carried on. By the end of the fourth round, Ali's eyes were burning. No one knows why but it is thought that the ointment used on Liston's cuts may have been applied to his gloves to deliberately blind his opponent. Ali survived the fifth round and the seat and tears removed the irritation from his eyes. That allowed him to return strong in the sixth round and hammered Liston with punches. Liston never returned for the seventh round, making Ali the winner. At just 22, he took the title from a reigning heavyweight champion, the youngest person to ever do so until 1986, when Mike Tyson broke his record.

It was shortly after this fight that Ali, still known as Clay, changed his name to Cassius X. Not long after that, he converted to Islam and changed his name to Muhammad Ali.

Unsurprisingly, it was the start of a winning streak, with some truly impressive fights along the way. One worth mentioning is the 1966 fight against Cleveland Williams, known as the hardest puncher in the heavyweight division. He didn't stand a chance against Ali as he danced his way around him and won a technical knockout in the third round. Many people have said it was Muhammad Ali's finest performance.

It should be noted that Ali lost four prime years of fighting due to his refusal to be inducted into the army for the Vietnam War. Ultimately, the court of appeals justified his stance. The process meant that Ali was stripped of his right to fight and his titles. He also faced jail. It made him a hero of those fighting for human rights and is said to have had a very positive effect on the human rights movement.

FUN FACTS ABOUT MUHAMMAD ALI

1. Ali was the first fighter to win the world heavyweight title on three separate occasions.
2. When he retired in 1981, he had 56 wins and just 5 losses (37 of the wins were KOs).
3. His first professional defeat was in March 1971 against Joe Frazier.
4. He beat Frazier six months later in a split decision to regain the heavyweight title.
5. His best friend was Howard Bingham a photographer.

QUICK TRIVIA TEST

What was Ali's birth name?

Cassius Marcellus Clay Jr.

What 1955 murder really affected the young Ali?

Emmett Till

Who first introduced him to boxing?

Police Officer Joe E. Martin

What age was he when he took the world heavyweight title from Sonny Liston?

22

Why did he refuse to serve in the Vietnam War?

His religion made him a conscientious objector

FIVE LIFE LESSONS

1. Don't let weaknesses hold you back

Ali had dyslexia. Today, this condition is recognized and there are options to help people manage with it. When Ali was young there was no such treatment. In fact, the condition wasn't really recognized. In other words, he was simply branded as stupid.

Ali didn't let this get him down. He fought through it and made something of himself, despite his weaknesses.

2. Create a persona

Ali was known as a big mouth because he was very vocal when trash-talking his opponents. This was a deliberate strategy for Ali as he tried to maximize crowd numbers. His ploy worked as crowd numbers were always highest when he was fighting.

You don't need to be a big mouth, but it's worth considering what persona could help you.

3. Nothing is impossible

While it may often seem like something is impossible, the truth is, nothing is impossible. Ali said it best when he said, "Impossible is potential, impossible is temporary, impossible is nothing."

If you try hard enough, you can achieve the impossible.

4. Make everything count

One of Ali's most famous phrases is "Float like a butterfly, sting like a bee, you can't hit what your eyes can't see." It effectively describes Ali in the ring. However, it can be used in all walks of life. You simply need to focus on creating a strategy that will allow you to deal with anything. Then seize every opportunity and make it count, having a strategy will make this easier.

5. Stand up for what you believe in

It can be difficult to stand against the crowd and remain true to your own beliefs. Ali did it when he decided to be a conscientious objector. It hurt his career and his reputation. It could have even seen him thrown in jail.

He stood up for what he believed in and was ultimately vindicated. Do the same and you'll reap the rewards.

MICHAEL PHELPS
SWIMMING

Put simply, Michael Phelps is the most decorated Olympian of all time. He has an amazing 28 medals. That includes 23 Olympic gold medals, which is an all-time record. He has a total of 16 Olympic medals in individual events. In 2004, he also achieved eight medals of any color, which meant he had tied the record with Olympic gymnast Alexander Dityatin.

Phelps was born in Baltimore, Maryland, in June 1985, and is the youngest of three children. As a young child, he had an excessive amount of energy. This caused his parents to sign him up for swimming classes, something that his sisters were already doing. His mom thought it would burn some of his energy and help him learn to swim. The young Phelps was just seven years old and instantly fell in love with swimming. It wasn't affected by his diagnosis of ADHD (Attention Deficit Hyperactivity Disorder). He learned various strokes and, by the time he was ten, he had earned a national record for the 100-meter butterfly. This led to him training under Bob Bowman at the North Baltimore Aquatic Club.

It's worth noting that his parents divorced when he was just nine years old. This led to a distant relationship with his father for several years. Phelps believes that the divorce had a negative effect on himself and his siblings.

Phelps trained with Bob Bowman since he turned 11 and it is the smartest move he could have made. The partnership worked as

Phelps rapidly got better and better at swimming. This allowed him to qualify for the 2000 Summer Olympics. He was just 15 at the time, the youngest male to reach the U.S. Olympic swim team since 1932! He made it to the finals and finished 5th in the 200-meter butterfly.

This turned out to be a warmup. The following year, he earned a spot in the World Championships. While at the trials, he set a new world record for the 200-meter butterfly. It made him the youngest male to ever set a world swimming record. He was just 15 years and 9 months old. During the actual event, he beat his own record and became the World Champion.

The 2002 national also went his way. He competed in the individual medley and set a new American record. He nearly got the world record in the 200-meter butterfly and beat the world record in the 400-meter individual medley. This was also the year he swam at the 2002 Pan Pacific Swimming Championships and earned three gold medals and two silvers.

In 2003, Phelps won the 200-meter freestyle, the 200-meter backstroke, and the 100-meter butterfly. This made him the first American to win three different races using different strokes at the national championship level. It was this year he broke the world record for the 400-meter medley and came within 0.03 seconds of beating the world record in the 100-meter butterfly. The same year, he broke the 200-meter individual medley.

The accolades continued. In the 2003 World Aquatics Championships, he won four gold medals and won silver medals. He also broke five world records.

In a testimony to his commitment to swimming, in the 2004 Summer Olympic trials, he competed in the 200- and 400-meter individual medleys, the 100- and 200-meter butterfly, the 200-meter backstroke, and the 200-meter freestyle. In trials, he won four and came second in two, despite there being just 30 minutes between some of the races! He was the first person to qualify for six individual events in the Olympics. Phelps chose to compete in five out of six categories. During the actual competition, Phelps won six gold medals and two bronze. He also set new world records for the 400-meter individual medley, the 200-meter butterfly, and the 200-meter individual medley.

In 2005, Phelps earned 5 golds and one silver at the 2005 Aquatics Championships, setting a new record for the 200-meter individual freestyle in the process. Another seven gold medals were added to his collection at the 2007 World Championships.

Unbelievably, the best was yet to come! In the 2008 Summer Olympics, Phelps earned eight gold medals. Seven of these were new world records. Eight gold medals at one Olympic Games was a new record, beating Mark Spritz's record of seven, which was set in 1972.

The list of golds and records goes on, even after his retirement! He officially retired in 2012 and then returned in 2014 to win three more golds and two silvers at the Pan Pacific Championships. In the 2016 Olympics, Phelps was 31 and getting old for a swimmer. Yet, he still managed five gold medals and one silver. In the last event of the 2016 Summer Olympics, Phelps and his team took gold in the 4 x 100-meter medley relay. The team broke the Olympic record and won the United States' 1001st all-time Summer Olympics gold medal. He then retired, feeling that he had achieved everything he could in the sport.

FUN FACTS ABOUT MICHAEL PHELPS

1. Phelps is very tall at 6ft 4.
2. He has set an impressive 39 world records.
3. The Michael Phelps Foundation helps young people learn about healthier lifestyles and the sport of swimming.
4. He loves playing golf.
5. Phelps signed up for Project Believe, meaning he was drug-tested more than the official guidelines required. He passed every test.

QUICK TRIVIA TEST

When was he born?

June 1985

How old was he when he qualified for the 2000 Summer Olympics?

15

Who was his coach for his entire career?

Bob Bowman

In what year did he win eight Olympic gold medals?

2008

How many world records has he set?

39

FIVE LIFE LESSONS

1. Aim high

Phelps once said, "Records are made to be broken no matter what they are. Anybody can do anything they set their mind to." If you prepare yourself mentally and physically, you can achieve anything. You simply need to aim high and be prepared to put in the work.

2. Never say never

Phelps retired in 2012 and then returned to the sport, proving you should never say never. While his motivation for returning isn't clear, the results don't lie. He returned and competed in events into his thirties, well past the prime for a swimmer, and still won a cluster of gold medals.

Think about that when you say "never again."

3. Visualization helps

Not all athletes swear by this. However, Phelps does. He says, "Other nights … I visualize to the point that I know exactly what I want to do: dive, glide, stroke, flip, reach the wall, hit the split time to the hundredth, then swim back again for as many times as I need to finish the race."

For Phelps, visualization helps his mind and body believe he has won before he starts, allowing him to give a winning performance. Try the same approach.

4. You can't always win

Phelps has won a lot of gold medals. However, he hasn't won every race he's entered. The simple truth is that this is virtually impossible. While you should always try your hardest to win, it's not always possible.

You can learn from the failures and the mistakes along the way, that's how you become a winner in the future. As Phelps says, "Things won't go perfect. It's all about how you adapt from those things and learn from mistakes."

5. Set your own goals

Phelps once said, "I have reached a place in my life where I need to sit down and say, 'Well, what do I do? What's best for me?' I need to look into options for the future."

This is something that everyone should do, whether you're at the start of a career, partway through, or looking for new options. It's important to take the time to decide what's best for you and set your goals accordingly.

USAIN BOLT
ATHLETICS

Usain St. Leo Bolt was born August 21, 1986, in Sherwood Content, a small town in Jamaica. His name was a suggestion from his mother's nephew-in-law and his middle name was provided by his aunt. Bolt has one brother and one sister. His childhood was fairly typical. While his parents ran the local grocery store, his brother and he would play cricket and football in the street. As he admits, he didn't really think about anything other than sports.

The young Bolt went to Waldensia Primary, where he was invited to take part in the annual national primary school meet. By the time he was 12, he was the fastest runner in the school. At this stage, he was developing a love for European soccer teams.

It was only when he attended high school that his cricket coach urged him to try track events. He had seen Bolt's speed. Fortunately, the school had a track record of success in athletics. Bolt was coached by Dwayne Jarrett and Pablo McNeil (a former Olympic sprint athlete). In 2001, at just 15, he took his first high school medal, a silver in the 200-meter race.

McNeil became his coach. However, Bolt was yet to take himself or his abilities seriously. He was a practical joker and even hid in the back of a van when he was supposed to be preparing for the 200-meter finals at the CARIFTA Trials. Despite this, he went to the CARIFTA Games and Bolt set records in the 200-meter and 400-meter.

It was the former Prime Minister, P.J. Patterson, who saw Bolt's talent and arranged for him to attend the Jamaica Amateur Athletic Association in Kingston. It gave Bolt the training that he needed.

In 2002, while he was still 15 and an impressive 6'5" tall, Bolt won the 200-meter race in 20.61 seconds. It was 0.03 seconds slower than his first-round time and Bolt discovered the effect of nerves. He vowed never to let them affect his performance again. He won four gold medals at the 2003 CARIFTA Games and was given the Austin Sealy Trophy for the most outstanding athlete.

Fascinatingly, Bolt beat the 200-meter and 400-meter records at his final Jamaican High school Championships, beating the old times by a significant amount. His times were starting to equal records. For example, at the Pan-American Junior Championships he ran the 200-meter in 20.13 seconds, matching Roy Martin's world junior record. However, he remained only partially focused on his career, frequently eating fast food, playing basketball, and partying.

The change happened in 2003 when he beat everyone in the trials for the Senior World Championships. But a bout of conjunctivitis ruined his training and he wasn't allowed to participate. This, and the arrival of a new coach, Fitz Coleman, helped him to take athletics more seriously.

At the 2004 CARIFTA Games, he became the first-ever junior sprinter to run the 200 meters in under 20 seconds! A hamstring injury ruined his 2004 World Junior Championships and got him eliminated in the first round of the 2004 Olympics.

The process of taking the sport more seriously may have started with Coleman, but it was cemented with Bolt's next coach, Glen Mills. After a good start to 2005, an injury in the final of the 2005 World Championships meant he finished in last place. The rest of that year and the next were injury-prone, hampering Bolt from producing his best performances. During this time, his coaches were pushing for him to run longer distances, Bolt set his heart on running a shorter one—the 100 meters. His coach finally said he could run the 100 meters if he beat the 200-meter national record. It certainly helped Bolt get serious! In the 2006 Jamaican Championships, he ran the 200 meters in 19.75 seconds, breaking the record which had been set by Don Quarrie 36 years before!

Following this, Bolt ran the 100 meters at the 23rd Vardinoyiannia meeting. In his first race, he won with a time of 10.03 seconds. Subsequently, he went to the 2007 World Championships and took the silver medal in the 200 meters with a run of 19.91 seconds.

Focus shifted to the 100 meters and Bolt ran 9.76 seconds in the Jamaica Invitational at Kingston. It was the second-fastest legal performance at this event. While Bolt was surprised, his coach knew he could be faster.

The Reebok Grand Prix was in May 2008 and Bolt set a new 100-meter world record with a time of 9.72 seconds. While his coach still liked the idea of Bolt competing in the 400-meter, the training schedule had improved his 100-meter and 200-meter times.

Finally, Bolt was ready to show his true abilities. In the 2008 Summer Olympics, he won the 100 meters in 9.69 seconds, setting a new world record. Best of all, he slowed down at the end to celebrate and had a shoelace untied. It was Jamaica's first gold medal of the 2008 Games. Bolt wasn't finished. He went on to win a gold medal in the 200-meter sprint and set another world record. He ran the 200-meter sprint in 19.3 seconds with a 0.9m/s headwind. He was the first sprinter to hold both 100-meter and 200-meter records since the start of electronic timing.

From that moment on, Bolt started to win more and more golds. He also started his now-famous lightning-bolt celebration move. It's justified, his list of medals is enviable. He has 8 Olympic gold medals, 11 World Championship golds, and has world records in the 100-meter and 200-meter sprints. He is also the only person to have won three gold medals in consecutive Olympics for the same event.

FUN FACTS ABOUT USAIN BOLT

1. While at the Olympic Games in Beijing, he ate approximately 1,000 chicken nuggets.
2. In 2009, he adopted a cheetah.
3. He loves playing *Call of Duty* on the PlayStation.
4. Bolt was born with scoliosis—an abnormal curvature of the spine.
5. He was first prompted to run by the promise of a box lunch at school.

QUICK TRIVIA TEST

What's Bolt's full name?

Usain St. Leo Bolt

When was he born?

August 21, 1986

Who arranged for him to go to Kingston?

Former Prime Minister, P.J. Patterson

How many Olympic gold medals does he have?

8

What did he have to do so that his coaches would let him try the 100-meter race?

Beat the 200-meter Jamaican national record

FIVE LIFE LESSONS

1. If you want to succeed, take it seriously

Although it wasn't obvious at the start, Bolt is a natural sprinter. However, while he recorded respectable times and was competitive, he didn't hit his form until he started to take the sport seriously.

The same is true in all walks of life, take the activity seriously, give it your all, and you'll reap the rewards.

2. Know your strengths

Bolt is technically too tall to be a sprinter. His height and long legs make it difficult for him to leave the blocks fast. At the start of a sprint you need short steps, that's hard with long legs. However, his long legs do allow him to take large strides which is perfect once he is out of the blocks. Bolt regularly reaches speeds of 28 mph.

He knows that his strength is the second two-thirds of the race and works hard to reduce the weakness of his start. That's what has made him such a good sprinter.

3. Give it your all

Bolt once said, "Worrying gets you nowhere. If you turn up worrying about how you're going to perform, you've already lost. Train hard, turn up, run your best and the rest will take care of itself."

It's true, focus on giving it your all, not on how well you'll perform.

4. You can't always win

Usain Bolt holds two world records. However, even he doesn't always win. As he says, "Being beaten is a wake-up call." It may not happen often but it's a great reminder that you can't be complacent. You must keep giving it your all.

5. Enjoy your success

When you've worked hard to succeed, there is no harm in enjoying the success. You still need to be focused on what's next, but you can take the time to enjoy your time. As Bolt says, "A lot of legends, a lot of people, have come before me. But this is my time."

BRUCE LEE
MARTIAL ARTS

Lee Jun-fan was born on November 27, 1940, in San Francisco. His parents both lived in Hong Kong but had traveled to San Francisco for an international opera tour. It meant that Lee Jun-fan, later known as Bruce Lee, was allowed to claim US citizenship.

At the age of four, his family returned to Hong Kong. His father was a Cantonese opera star and Lee was first carried onto the stage as a boy in *Golden Gate Girl*—he was no stranger to the movies! As a child, he appeared in several films and then, at age nine, he co-starred with his father in *The Kid*. It was 1950 and his first leading role. He starred in 20 films before he was 18!

He started at school at 12 and got into several street fights. This is when his parents decided he should learn martial arts. The school boxing coach taught him several things and then, in 1953, he was introduced to Ip Man. Unfortunately, he wasn't allowed to learn Wing Chun Kung Fu because the European background on his mother's side classified him as a foreigner. Fortunately, his friend spoke up for him and he was accepted into the school. He encountered problems because most of the other students refused to train with him. Lee trained privately with Ip Man, Lee's friend William Cheung, and Wong Shun-leung.

Despite the discipline that martial arts were trying to teach him, Lee continued to get into fights. At one point, he beat a boy so badly that the police said another complaint would mean he would have to go to jail. Subsequently, when he turned 18, they sent him to San Francisco to live with family friends. He continued his education while teaching Jun Fan Gung Fu (Bruce Lee's Kung Fu). He opened several studios. It was around this time, 1964, that he demonstrated the one-inch punch. He punched volunteer Bob Baker from one-inch away sending him flying backward. Baker later commented that he had to stay home from work because the pain was unbearable.

This was the same year he had a private match with Wong Jack-man. The match was controversial as, according to rumors, it was organized by the Chinese community to stop Lee from teaching. Of course, there are no definitive stories regarding what happened and who won the fight.

At this stage, Lee was focused on teaching martial arts and was no longer involved in making movies. However, one of his many martial arts exhibitions in Long Beach was seen by a television producer, William Dozier, and he asked him to audition for the role of Lee Chan. That show never happened. However, from 1966 to 1970, Bruce lee played Kato in the *Green Hornet*. It was the first time that Asian martial arts were shown to an American audience. The show proved to be popular. Initially, Lee was told to use fists and punches in the American style. Lee refused, citing the fact he was a professional martial artist. The production company relented but Lee moved so fast that the camera couldn't capture his movements.

It was at this time that Lee developed his own style of fighting. No matter what had happened in his fight with Wong Jack-man, Lee felt that he had been too slow, the fight had taken too long, and he didn't achieve his full potential. To rectify this, Lee decided to develop a new style of martial arts that would be more practical in street fights. His system emphasized practicality, flexibility, efficiency, and speed. Alongside developing the new technique, Lee focused on weight training to build strength, running to increase endurance, stretching to maximize flexibility, and an array of other activities. He sculpted each one to match his needs. In essence, he developed a style with no limitations sitting outside the existing martial arts parameters.

As luck would have it, two of his students were in Hollywood—one was a scriptwriter, the other an actor. The two of them worked with Lee to create a script, although it never made it to movie screens. Lee was becoming known in Hollywood and was starting to get parts, such as playing a hoodlum in *The Silent Flute*. However, thanks to his ethnicity and accent, he couldn't secure any major roles. At the time, he was offered a film role by producer Fred Weintraub in Hong Kong. He returned to Hong Kong and found that the *Green Hornet* had been renamed *The Kato Show*. He was recognized as the star of the show.

By 1971, he was starring in his own movies. Specifically, the three films *The Big Boss*, *Fist of Fury*, and *The Way of the Dragon*. All three films were commercial success and made Lee a huge star. Shortly after this, he came back to the States to film *Enter the Dragon*. It was one of the year's biggest-grossing films. Naturally, the film sparked a massive interest in martial arts, especially after Lee's unexpected and untimely death.

Lee is often seen as the ultimate fighter. He learned a variety of martial arts, including Northern Praying Mantis, Southern Praying Mantis, Eagle Claw, Tan Tui, Law Hon, Mizongyi, Wa K'ung, Monkey, Southern Dragon, Fujian White Crane, Choy Li Fut, Hung Gar, Choy Gar, Fut Gar, Mok Gar, Yau Kung Moon, Li Gar, and Lau Gar.

Bruce Lee is responsible for the one-inch punch, the oblique kick, and the accupunch. Importantly, Lee was always looking outside the norms. He trained with different judo practitioners, learned wrestling, and added elements of his experience of street fighting in Hong Kong. He also studied nutrition and favored Asian cuisine even when living in the States.

Bruce Lee may never have won an Olympic gold or any competition; however, he did revolutionize martial arts and made them accessible to all. However, his status as legendary comes from the various videos and films showing his fighting style. He was fluid, fast, and deadly, potentially the greatest martial artist to ever live.

FUN FACTS ABOUT BRUCE LEE

1. Lee won a High School boxing tournament in Hong Kong.
2. He mentored Kareem Abdul Jabbar, partly inspiring him to play basketball.
3. Lee opened his first martial arts school when he was just 20 years old.
4. He was only 5'6" tall.
5. Bruce Lee had two children with his wife Linda before he died.

QUICK TRIVIA TEST

What was Lee's birth name?

Lee Jun-fan

Why was he allowed American citizenship?

Because he was born in San Francisco

Why was he sent back to the US at 18?

Because he was having too many street fights in Hong Kong

When was he introduced to Ip Man?

1953

What did his fight with Wong Jack-man make him realize?

That a new form of martial arts was needed

FIVE LIFE LESSONS

1. Choose your own path

Bruce Lee was incredibly fast, it was one of the reasons he excelled at martial arts. However, he wasn't satisfied with the martial arts forms on offer and created his own. It took time, an understanding of various fighting techniques, and a lot of courage as he faced resistance from China.

For him, it was worth it.

2. Seize the day

Bruce Lee sadly died when he was just 32. By then, he had created his own style of martial arts, become a box office success, and was even directing his own movies. No one could have predicted he would die that day, emphasizing why you should seize any opportunity. You simply don't know when it will be your time.

3. Be open to anything

Lee used to say "Be like water, my friend." Water flows around and through any obstacle in its path. Lee was suggesting that people should adopt the same attitude in life. You don't need to destroy what's in your way, simply flow round and through it.

In life, this means don't get trapped in a certain mindset, adapt to what is going on around you.

4. Anything is possible

Lee once said, "When you say that something is impossible, you have made it impossible." He achieved a lot in his short life because he was open to what was possible. You should adopt the same approach. If you believe anything is possible, you'll be surprised at what you can achieve.

5. Accept failure

As Lee said, "Everyone wants to learn how to win, but no one wants to learn how to accept defeat." While there are times when failure simply isn't an option, in many cases, failure is simply an opportunity to learn and do better the next time.

You have to learn to except and embrace your failures, only then can you be a true winner.

MIKE TYSON
BOXING

Mike Gerald Tyson was born June 30, 1966, in Fort Greene, Brooklyn. He has one older brother and an older sister who sadly died of a heart attack at just 24 years old. Tyson had a tough childhood. His father left around the time he was born and his mother struggled financially. It meant they lived in the poorest and roughest neighborhoods. By the time he turned 13, Tyson had been arrested 38 times. In an effort to straighten him out, he was sent to the Tryon School for Boys. It was there that a juvenile detention center counselor and former boxer, Booby Stewart, noticed Tyson's ability to box. Stewart trained Tyson for several months before introducing him to Cus D'Amato, a boxing manager and trainer. He became Tyson's guardian when he was 16 and his mother died.

The training worked because Tyson made it to the junior Olympic team and won gold at the 1981 and 1982 Junior Olympic Games. He beat Joe Cortez in 1981 and Kelton Brown in 1982. However, it wasn't all glory. Although he beat Jonathan Littles to secure the National Golden Gloves, he lost twice to Henry Tillman as an amateur.

He turned professional and had his first professional fight on March 6, 1985. His opponent was Hector Mercedes and Tyson scored a win based on a technical knockout in the first round. Tyson went on to fight 15 times in his first professional year. Impressively, 26 of his first 28 fights were won by way of a knockout.

Tyson was rapidly rising up the rankings and, by July, had secured a fight against former world title challenger Mavis Frazier. The fight was short, Tyson charged Fraizer as soon as the bell rang and hit him with two uppercuts. The second of these knocked Fraizer out, ending the fight in less than 30 seconds.

In November 1986, Tyson fought Trevor Berbick for the World Boxing Council heavyweight championship title. He knocked out Berbick in the second round and became the youngest heavyweight champion in history, knocking Muhammad Ali off the top spot. Interestingly, Ali made mincemeat of Sonny Liston, who is deemed to be the most intimidating man in boxing history, and Tyson based his boxing style on Liston, which makes you wonder how Tyson would fare against Ali.

Between 1987 and 1990, Tyson reigned supreme. He was the undisputed king of the heavyweight boxing world and, during that time, he never took a step back or met a challenger that created a serious issue for him. He earned a knockout-to-win ratio of 88% and ESPN listed him top on their list of "The Hardest Hitters in Heavyweight History."

While Tyson has had his fair share of problems outside the ring, he is also charged with restoring glory to the sport of boxing. His presence boosted interest in boxing by fan numbers and by encouraging more people to take up the sport.

In August 1987, Tyson became the first heavyweight boxer to have all three major titles, the WBA, WBC, and the IBF, simultaneously. His style and the power of his punch led Nintendo to release *Mike Tyson's Punch-Out!!!* The game sold exceptionally well.

However, 1988 was perhaps Tyson's greatest year. He only fought three times. The first one was against Larry Holmes, a legend in his own right. Tyson knocked out Holmes in the fourth round, it was the only time Holmes had ever been knocked out in 75 professional fights. Another testimony to the power of Iron Mike. The second fight was against Tony Tubbs, Tyson knocked him out in the second round.

In June of the same year, Tyson fought Michael Spinks. He had beaten Holmes in a 15-round fight to gain the IBF heavyweight title. It was taken off him as he refused to fight the number one contender. However, most people considered Spinks to have a claim as the heavyweight champion. The fight was expected to be spectacular—two titans slogging it out, Tyson aggressive and fast, Spinks skill at out-boxing and fancy footwork. Unfortunately for Spinks, Tyson knocked him out just 91 seconds into the first round.

Tyson has faced a lot of personal issues since those dominant years, and that's why his career peak is so short. However, during that period, he was the most intimidating boxer on the planet and the power of his punch hasn't been matched before or since. Tyson regularly comes in the top ten of the best heavyweights ever. It's likely that he would be ranked in the first two if not for personal issues causing problems in the ring.

In 2011, Tyson was inducted into the International Boxing Hall of Fame. As he gets older, he's managing to put life more into perspective. In 2012, he launched the Mike Tyson Cares Foundation. The foundation helps children from broken homes by meeting their physical and mental needs.

In his career, he fought 58 professional fights and won 50 of them. Staggeringly, 44 of those wins were knockouts, testifying to the power of Iron Mike's punch.

FUN FACTS ABOUT MIKE TYSON

1. Tyson has appeared in several films, such as *The Hangover*.
2. He retired in 2005, made a comeback in 2020, and is scheduled to fight again in 2024.
3. His fight against Evander Holyfield ended in disqualification after Tyson bit part of Holyfield's ear off.
4. Tyson loves pigeon racing.
5. His 91-second knockout of Spinks is the fastest knockout in a heavyweight title fight ever.

QUICK TRIVIA TEST

What is Tyson's full name?

Mike Gerald Tyson

When did he start boxing professionally?

1985

How old was he when he won the heavyweight championship?

20

How fast did he knockout Spinks in the 1988 heavyweight title fight?

91 seconds

When was he inducted into the International Hall of Fame?

2011

FIVE LIFE LESSONS

1. Never quit!

Tyson had it tough growing up and got into a lot of trouble. His energy and speed eventually translated into fighting power, making him one of the greatest boxers ever and deserving of legendary status. The key to his success is simply never quitting.

No matter how hard he went down, in or out of the ring, he always got back up and tried again. It's a good approach to life.

2. Find your own peace

When Tyson was young there was much less understanding of mental strength than there is today. If Tyson had made peace with his past and built a positive mental attitude, he could have remained at the peak of his sport for many more years.

Whatever you try to do in life, it's worth looking after your mental health and finding your own peace. It will help you become more successful.

3. Dare to dream

Tyson once said, "I'm a dreamer. I have to dream and reach for the stars, and if I miss a star then I grab a handful of clouds." Everyone has different dreams but you need to have a dream if you want to succeed in life.

4. You can't always win

As a professional boxer, Tyson experienced his first loss in 1990. He was the heavyweight champion of the world and his opponent, Buster Douglas, shouldn't have stood a chance. Douglas won the fight because Tyson didn't prepare properly.

However, afterward, he was grateful because it made him realize he had taken his skill for granted. As he once said, "In order to succeed greatly, you have to be prepared to fail greatly. If you can't do both of them, you've got a problem."

5. Push your limits

The only way to achieve anything in life is to push your limits. Getting outside your comfort zone means you learn and expand as an individual. That's essential throughout life. As Tyson once said, "You have to feel comfortable being uncomfortable. I'm always comfortable being uncomfortable. And to be comfortable being uncomfortable, I have to hone my discipline, which to me is doing what I have to do, but also doing it like I love it."

DON BRADMAN
CRICKET

Sir Don Bradman was born in August 1908 in Cootamundra, New South Wales, Australia. It wasn't known at the time, but he was destined for greatness. Even today, over 100 years later, he is seen as the greatest batsman of all time.

He's the youngest of five, having one older brother and three older sisters. Although born in Australia, his heritage was English. In fact, his grandfather Charles Andrew Bradman had moved from Suffolk, England, to Australia. His mother was also a keen cricketer. She was a bowler with a left-arm spin and played women's intercolonial cricket throughout the 1890s. It was her love of cricket that led Bradman to start.

As a youngster, he practiced every day. Without anyone to practice with, it's said that he used a cricket stump for a bat and a golf ball. He would hit the ball against a curved water tank as hard as possible. Thanks to the curve of the tank, it was difficult to know where the ball would go. He honed his reactions by trying to hit the rebound. This practice is often cited as the reason why his timing was so accurate and his reactions so fast.

Naturally, he started to play cricket at school and, at the age of 12, he scored his first century. In fact, he scored 115 not out in a game between his school, Bowral Public School, and another local school, Mittagong High School. It was at this time he started to act as scorer for the local Bowral team and even played when the team was short a man. This was also when his father took him to see the fifth Ashes Test match. Bradman declared, "I shall never be satisfied until I play on this ground."

At just 14, Bradman left school and started working for a local estate agent. They gave him time off as necessary to play sports. Strangely, considering Bradman's dream of playing at Sydney Cricket Ground, he gave up cricket for two years and played tennis for two years instead.

He returned to the game in 1925 and became a regular on the Bowral team. His performances earned him rave reviews in the papers. Of particular note was his 234 against Wingello and an impressive 320 not out in the competition final against Moss Vale. It was during the winter of 1926 that the New South Wales Cricket Association wrote to him and asked him to attend practice. The Australian cricket team was aging and replacements were needed. He was actually invited to play tennis and cricket. However, they were on separate weeks and his job could only let him have one week off. He chose cricket and, thanks to his performance, he was invited to play grade cricket.

In his first turf game, he scored 110 and every Saturday he would travel 130 kilometers from Bowral to Sydney to play for the NSW second team, St. George. The following season he was moved to the first team. His first match was at the Adelaide Oval and he scored 118. It was instantly apparent that pressure didn't bother him. He had fast footwork, was calm, confident, and scored rapidly. Shortly after, he played at the Sydney Cricket Ground against the Sheffield Shield Champions, Victoria, and scored his first century at the ground.

He moved to Sydney to improve his chances of making the Australian Test team; England was due to tour to defend their Ashes win. In his first game of the season, he scored a century against Queensland and got his chance to play against England, scoring 87 and 132 not out.

He got his chance but found his first test much harder than expected. He was caught on a sticky wicket and Australia were all out for 66 in the second innings. They lost by a record-setting 675. It was the incentive Bradman needed. Initially, he was dropped from the team but made it back as a substitute. He played in the third Test at Melbourne and scored 79 and 112, making him the youngest player to ever score a century in a Test.

In the second innings, Bradman was run out, the only time it ever happened in his career! But his revitalized style had a positive effect on the team. They managed to win the Fifth and final Test. He scored 123 and was at the wicket when the team captain scored the winning runs. It was the year he set the record for a multiple century in a Shield match without being knocked out.

His success grew, he played in a trial match to determine the team that would tour England. He was the last batsman and ended the first innings with 124 not out. His captain, Bill Woodfull, asked him to open the second innings and he went on to score 225 not out. He continued the run at Queensland and managed 452 not out, setting a new world record!

The 1930s Ashes were expected to be won by England. Australia had two promising batsmen—Bradman and Jackson. While Jackson appeared to be the greater talent, it was Bradman who started the tour with 236 at Worcester and became the first Australian to score 1,000 first-class runs by the end of May. In his first test, he hit 131 in the second innings, although England still won. In the second test, he scored 254, giving Australia the victory. On the third Test he scored 100 before lunch, 100 before tea, and finished the day on 309 not out. The deciding Test was played over three days due to poor weather. Bradman scored 232 and his partnership with Jackson meant Australia took the game and the Test.

The victory turned Bradman into a hero. He was the boy from the bush who taught himself cricket and beat Australia's oldest rival. Most of the records he set during that Test are still standing today. It's fair to say, despite many impressive achievements since his legend was born during that Test.

FUN FACTS ABOUT DON BRADMAN

1. Bradman captained the Australian team in 1936, they won all 36 matches.
2. He wrote the book *The Art of Cricket*.
3. Bradman is the only Australian cricketer to be knighted—it took place in 1949, the year he retired.
4. His batting average was 99.94, no one else has ever come close to this.
5. There's a statue of Sir Donald Bradman, known affectionately as "The Don" outside the Adelaide cricket ground. It's 2.5-meters tall.

QUICK TRIVIA TEST

When was Bradman born?

August 1908

How many brothers and sisters does he have?

4 (all older)

How old was he when he scored his first century?

Twelve

What did he play when he took a break from cricket?

Tennis

Why did he move to Sydney?

To improve the possibility of being selected for the Test team

FIVE LIFE LESSONS

1. Everyone should have a dream

Bradman dreamed of playing at Sydney Cricket Ground in the Ashes from when he was 12 years old. It was a dream he clung too and eventually made come true. Everyone should have a dream because it gives you a purpose in life.

2. Consider others

After winning the 1930s Test against England, Bradman became a national hero and was asked to tour Australia to boost the image of cricket. Bradman did but later said, "It permanently damaged relationships with his contemporaries."

He was right, cricket is a team game, not an individual one. Consider your teammates in everything you do.

3. You can learn anything if you want

Bradman once said, "I was never coached, I was never even taught how to hold a bat." Despite this, he became the greatest batsman the sport has ever known. That's proof that you can do anything if you put your mind to it.

4. Modesty is a good attribute

There is no harm in owning your victories. However, you can also be modest and acknowledge the prowess and success of others. Bradman used to say, "Many cricketers who had more ability than I had. Why they didn't make more runs than I did, I don't know."

5. Think about the greater good

Bradman was reserved, almost shy. However, he recognized how good some things were for the game even if he didn't want them. For example, he said about his knighthood, "About the last thing I ever wanted in life was a knighthood, and even today some forty years after the event, I find it difficult to come to terms with a life where old and valued friends insist on calling me 'Sir' instead of Don, simply because they think it is protocol. But I have consciously shouldered these burdens because I felt that I was the medium through which cricket could achieve a higher status and gain maximum support from the people, not only in Australia but throughout the world."

Sometimes, you have to do things you're not comfortable with for the greater good. That's worth remembering.

DALEY THOMPSON
ATHLETICS

Daley Thompson was born Francis Morgan Ayodele Thompson in July 1958. He went on to win a gold medal in the 1980 and 1984 Olympic Games in the decathlon event. He broke the World Record four times and was unbeaten in competition for an impressive nine years. His total medal haul includes four world records, two Olympic Golds, three Commonwealth titles, World Championship wins, and European Championship victories. He is generally regarded as the greatest decathlete to ever live.

Thompson was born in the Notting Hill area of London. His father was a cab driver but left his family when Thompson was just six. Although he doesn't remember much from this period, when he was seven, his mother sent him to Farney Close Boarding School, which is best described as a place for troubled children. As a child, he loved kicking a ball around and aspired to become a professional soccer player. However, he tried athletics and found that he enjoyed it.

In 1975, he joined the Newham and Essex Beagles Athletic Club. He started out as a sprinter but his coach recommended that he try the decathlon. Thompson did and later in the same year entered his first competition. It was a decathlon in Cwmbran, Wales, and Thompson won. He won his next competition and then in 1976, the AAA title, followed by being placed 18th at the Montreal Olympic Games.

This inspired Thompson. In 1978, he won the European Junior title and the Commonwealth title (the first of three times he won this). Strangely, in 1979, he only entered one decathlon and failed to finish. However, he did win the long jump at the UK Championships. Despite this, he was selected for the Olympic team and gained 8,648 points at Gotzis in Austria, setting a world record in the process. He went on to take the gold at the Moscow Olympics.

In 1982, he was again at Gotzis and beat his own world record, scoring an impressive 8,730 points. This obviously wasn't good enough for him. In September of the same year, he scored 8,774 points, creating yet another world record. In October, he retook the Commonwealth title.

In 1983, he won the World Championships and became the first person to hold both the European and World titles at the same time. Thompson spent much of 1984 preparing for the Olympics. He was expecting Jurgen Hingsen, the current world record holder, to be a serious threat. However, Thompson took the lead in the first event and went on to comfortably win another Olympic gold. This was also the year the new scoring tables were introduced, making Thompson the record holder with his score of 8,847 points. His performance at the 1984 Olympics has yet to be beaten.

In 1986, he won his third and final Commonwealth title. He also won the European Championship but his edge was starting to slip. By 1987, he suffered his first defeat in nine years and, although he attended the 1990 Commonwealth Games, he couldn't compete due to an injury.

Throughout the late 1980s, Thompson and Hingsen constantly traded the world record between them. Yet, despite the intense rivalry and apparent similarities, Daley never lost a competition between 1978 and 1987. He was simply better on the day every time.

FUN FACTS ABOUT DALEY THOMPSON

1. Since retiring, he has become a successful motivational speaker and fitness trainer.
2. Thompson was awarded with an MBE in 1983 and a CBE in 2000.
3. He was known to train relentlessly.
4. His name was used by Ocean Software for three official computer games in the 1980s.
5. Thompson used to appear in Lucozade adverts.

QUICK TRIVIA TEST

What was Thompson's birth name?

Francis Morgan Ayodele Thompson

When was he born?

July 1958

How many Olympic golds did he win?

Two

What is Thompson's world record point score?

8,847

Why did he not win a fourth Commonwealth Championship?

An injury forced him to withdraw

FIVE LIFE LESSONS

How you perform on the day matters

Every athlete has their own routine to ensure maximum performance when it counts. While Thompson hasn't shared what he did before an event, whatever it was clearly gave him the edge over his rival Hingsen.

You need to evaluate what puts you in the right space physically and mentally and make sure you're ready, whatever the event.

Training ensures success

Thompson was well known for being committed to training. He was relentless, frequently creating punishing training schedules and sticking to them. It was part of his drive for perfection and definitely contributed to his success.

At the time, his determination and discipline regarding training set him apart from all his competitors.

Commit!

To achieve success in almost anything in life you have to commit to the activity. It's not always easy to commit, you need to be mentally and physically ready. But, as Thompson once said, "If you're not in it, you can't win it."

Get the right mental attitude

Winning is as much about having the right mental attitude as it is about being physically ready. You need to start thinking positively, building confidence in your own actions, and believing that you can, and will, win.

As Thompson says, "The only limitations are mental. The guy who thinks positively will win."

Remember your weaknesses

It's generally easier to work on your strengths, that's things you're already good at or enjoy doing. It's much harder to work on your weak areas. However, to give your best performance and win, you need to work harder on your weaknesses and turn them into strengths.

As Thompson says, "Sometimes you have to resist working on your strengths in favor of your weaknesses. The decathlon requires a wide range of skills."

SABINA ALTYNBEKOVA
VOLLEYBALL

Sabina Altynbekova was born on November 5, 1996, and is young to be a legend! She was born in Aktobe, Kazakhstan, and lived a fairly normal childhood. Although she enjoyed sports, she didn't start playing volleyball until she was 14 years old. Her talent was obvious.

Altynbekova found that she loved playing volleyball and dedicated time to practicing, trying to improve her game, and becoming the best possible player. She joined club teams that allowed her to compete in local and even national tournaments. While she performed well, her profile was sufficiently elevated to attract attention until 2014. That's when she was selected to play in the Asian U19 Volleyball Championship. This was a widely publicized event and brought Altynbekova a lot more attention. Although her team performance was average, spectators and the media noted how effective she was at getting to and controlling the ball. Practically overnight she became famous. She was just 17.

Thanks to the power of social media, photos and videos of her went viral and she quickly became known across the globe. It's a testimony to the power of the modern internet. This could have influenced her actions or even taken her away from volleyball. However, she chose to keep focused on the game and on her training.

By 2015, she had several offers on the table and chose to sign with Dentsu, a Japanese sports agency. She was the first foreign member of the agency. She played in the Japan Challenge League II for several months before heading to Dubai. She signed with the Al-Wasl club and played with them for the remainder of the season, broadening her skills and experience. Since then, she has returned to Kazakhstan and is now part of the Kazakhstan women's national volleyball team.

The team continues to perform well, although not as well as some other countries. They have gained 5th place in the Asian Championships and 5th place in the Asian Games. They even secured a silver medal in the Asian Cup and the same in the Asian Challenge Cup. The team has also earned a silver medal in the CAVA Challenge Cup, a testimony to how they are still improving.

It may not strike you as legendary. However, there is more to this story than meets the eye. Her explosion on social media has put Altynbekova in direct contact with a host of A-list celebrities, such as Miranda Kerr and soccer legend Luis Figo. Her follower numbers have gone through the roof, she passed the one-million milestone on her 24th birthday. In short, she has found a stage where she can express her thoughts, feelings, and desires.

Altynbekova is using these platforms to elevate awareness of volleyball, particularly in places where it hasn't traditionally been a sport. In short, her popularity is translating into a dramatic increase in interest from young people wanting to get into the sport. Continuing to play and perhaps break records is difficult. As her coach says "It is impossible to work like this. The crowd behaves like there is only one player at the game." Audience numbers have risen dramatically, a direct result of Altynbekova's presence. But, if the audience is only there to see her, this can be distracting for the rest of the team. That's why her playtime was reduced to very little.

Unfortunately, the situation reached a head in 2019 and Altynbekova found herself without a club. She's dedicated herself to making the game more accessible to young volleyball players, especially young girls wishing to emulate her success. Her legendary status, despite being so young, comes from her willingness to adapt and give back to the game. Specifically, she's changing the way it is viewed and using her status to increase the popularity of volleyball.

It's a challenging role for someone who just wants to play volleyball, but it's one that she is committed to. In addition, Altynbekova's success has helped Kazakhstan showcase its rich heritage, its deep-seated culture, and the amount of talent that they have available.

FUN FACTS ABOUT SABINA ALTYNBEKOVA

1. Altynbekova went to a boarding school for gifted children.
2. She was just 17 when she played in the now-infamous tournament.
3. Altynbekova is 6' 1" tall, which is an advantage on the court.
4. Her father also played for the Kazakhstan team.
5. She's already worth an estimated £5 million.

QUICK TRIVIA TEST

When was Altynbekova born?

November 5, 1996

Where was she born?

Aktobe, Kazakhstan

How old was she when she started to play volleyball?

14

What competition pushed her into the public eye?

The Asian U19 Volleyball Championships

Why is it difficult for her to play volleyball now?

Because the focus is on her and not the rest of the team

FIVE LIFE LESSONS

1. Be true to yourself

It's easy to get caught up in the moment, especially when your social media following explodes overnight. Many people would be happy to take this following and turn it into a cash generator. However, Altynbekova simply wants to play volleyball and has remained true to her goal.

It's a good idea to be true to yourself and your dreams, you're more likely to end up happy.

2. Understand how you can make a difference

Altynbekova stated that she just wanted to play volleyball. However, even she appreciates that her star status can help her reach and encourage people who may otherwise not push their limits or reach for the stars.

When you understand that fame allows you to make a difference to others, you'll know how to use it to improve other people's lives.

3. Fame doesn't last forever

The key reason to do something you love as opposed to something that pays well or will make you famous is because the latter things don't last. Fame and money can both disappear practically overnight.

Today, Altynbekova isn't as famous as she was in 2014, but she's still doing what she loves and may yet get the chance to create new records. Fame doesn't last forever, but your passion does.

4. Make the most of what you have

Altynbekova is a talented volleyball player and simply wants to play. However, the amount of publicity surrounding her makes this difficult. While she wants to return to competitive play and enhance the reputation of volleyball in Kazakhstan, she has made the most of the opportunities presented to her. This includes maintaining contact with her fans, launching a fashion line, and various other endeavors.

In other words, she's making the most of the opportunities presented to her.

5. Don't believe everything you see

Altynbekova is living proof that not everything in print is true. In the first instance, there are multiple social media accounts professing to be hers. She has publicly stated she only uses Instagram and that people should avoid other social media accounts pretending to be hers.

The simple truth is that social media has made it very easy to manipulate the truth, you can't believe everything you read online.

BONUS MATERIAL SPORTS LEGENDS

HUNDRED AFFIRMATIONS TO BUILD CONFIDENCE

Confidence is key to success and success builds confidence. It sounds like a circle that can be tough to break into. The good news is you can start building confidence right now. It's easier than you think, simply choose some affirmations and repeat them daily. You'll start to believe what you're saying and it will make a difference to your confidence and your life.

Choose some of the following and repeat them every day, or repeat different ones and work your way through the list. Either approach can work, it's what suits you better.

- My opinions are important
- I am worth listening to
- I am mentally strong
- I have feelings that matter
- I'm a good person
- Anything is possible if you try hard enough
- A positive mindset can help you achieve the impossible
- I face one fear every day
- I am who I am and that's a good thing
- I love myself

- I'm worthy of respect
- I'm a good soccer player
- I can learn anything
- I'm prepared to stand up for what I believe in
- Everyone makes mistakes, I learn from mine
- I can overcome any obstacle
- I make good decisions
- I trust myself
- I am confident
- I am good at solving problems
- I'm a natural leader
- I don't follow others blindly but choose my own path
- I will succeed
- I trust my own instincts
- I focus on learning something new daily
- I see the positive in everyone and everything
- I always look for the joy in life
- Everyone has a good side
- Opportunities are everywhere, and I'm ready to seize them
- Every morning I look in the mirror and smile
- I'm a great listener
- I'm curious about everything, and that's a good thing
- I try to make someone smile every day
- I'm good at helping others
- I'm patient with others
- I'm kind to others
- Embracing change is a good thing
- I don't need to fill the silence with noise
- I always pause to consider my actions before acting
- I take time to exercise daily
- Practicing soccer daily is important to me
- I am ready and able to learn something new

- I will persevere, no matter what the obstacles are
- I make friends easily
- I appreciate criticism as a chance to grow mentally and physically
- Putting my friends first is important to me
- Everyone is worthy in their way
- Other people usually like me straight away
- I'm happy to share with others
- I play well in a team
- I can make a difference
- My body is perfect, just the way it is
- I appreciate the natural beauty in the world around me
- I can recover from any setback
- I'm great at solving problems
- I can think outside the box
- I always treat others how I would like to be treated
- Nothing is impossible
- I'm passionate about learning new skills
- I can always grow as a person
- I'm excited about future prospects
- I'm good at setting, and then achieving, goals
- I understand and embrace my feelings
- I'm capable of calming myself when angry
- I learn from my mistakes without dwelling on the past
- Every day is full of new and exciting prospects
- I smile at everyone I meet
- I'm grateful for what I have
- I'm confident
- I am proud of what I have achieved
- I display empathy for others
- I choose to be happy
- Learning is a gift I unwrap every day

- I'm a positive influence on everyone around me
- I'm always open to new ideas
- I'm intelligent
- I stand up for others
- I'm capable of defending my own opinions and actions
- I can make my dreams come true
- I am important
- I make good decisions
- I know the difference between right and wrong
- I can handle responsibility
- I'm a good role model
- I understand the importance of boundaries and respect them
- I like to include others
- I'm a good team player
- I believe curiosity is a blessing
- I'm open to anything
- I can be a great leader
- I am appreciative of others
- I make good things happen
- I believe generosity will be rewarded
- I enjoy helping others even when others don't appreciate my help
- I trust my own instincts
- Every opportunity is a bonus
- I'm a great friend
- I'm not perfect but nobody is
- I have a fantastic personality
- I know the importance of taking a break

THE MENTAL MINDSET
TO HELP YOU BECOME A LEGEND

As so many great athletes, legends, and famous businesspeople have said, talent is not enough for success. You need a plan to ensure you're at the top of your game physically and mentally. The physical challenge to becoming a legend is ensuring your body is in great shape and proofing it as much as possible against injury. This is achieved through practice. That doesn't just mean playing your chosen sport, you should practice an array of other exercises to help strengthen your physique for your chosen sport.

Mental preparation is often overlooked but is equally, if not more important. Fortunately, there are several things that you can do to help you develop the right mental mindset. It's never too soon to start as the right mental mindset will help you in all elements of life, whatever you plan to do. Here's what you need to do.

Start Using Affirmations

We've provided you with 100 affirmations, start using them! Equally, you can create your own affirmations. The aim is to repeat several every morning. You can repeat them throughout the day. By telling yourself something positive every day, you'll start to believe it is true. That will change your mindset from thinking something may be possible to believing it is not only possible but that you can achieve it.

The trick is to choose affirmations that focus on your weaknesses. It's these that you need to put the most effort into. Spend a little time considering your weaknesses both physically and mentally, then choose, or create, affirmations that will target these weaknesses.

After a few weeks, the affirmations will become a habit and you'll be surprised at how quickly they can change the way you feel about your performance and abilities.

Create a Sleep Plan

Your next step to becoming a legend is to create a sleep plan. All the biggest stars are committed to getting enough sleep. Becoming a legend is physically demanding. Your body needs time to recover and repair muscle damage. It does this while you sleep.

This is also the time that your mind rests, processes the thoughts of the day, and allows you to find the right way forward. Create a sleep schedule that allows you to get enough sleep, around eight hours is a good starting point.

As part of your sleep schedule, create a sleep plan. This is the time you go to bed and the process of shutting your mind and body down ready for sleep. For instance, turning off screens an hour before bed, perhaps reading or listening to music, and dimming the lights. You'll find you get to sleep easier and sleep better.

Schedule Your Sport

If you're passionate about a specific sport, or sport in general, then you'll probably want to do it all the time. While this can seem like a great way to practice and improve, this approach is more likely to leave you feeling tired. In short, your game is likely to suffer. If you don't play as well as you want, you're likely to feel frustrated and this can affect your state of mind.

A better approach is to play when you feel like it for fun, and schedule time for specific practice. Adopting this approach allows you to prepare yourself mentally and physically for each sport session. You'll find it easier to focus on what you want to improve and more rewarding.

In turn, this will help you feel confident about your chosen sport and your skill level. It will be a benefit to you physically and mentally.

Of course, you should always listen to your mind and body. If you're getting tired take a break, you'll come back stronger.

Visualizations

Many legendary sportspeople, such as Michael Phelps and Michael Jordan, use visualization. You'll also find many celebrities, such as Will Smith and Jay Z, do the same.

Visualization effectively means imagining what will happen throughout any given activity. It doesn't matter if you're boxing, playing basketball, or even giving a speech. You simply imagine what you want and believe will happen. Of course, you need to focus your visualization on what's in your control, such as scoring a goal or basket. According to studies, people who visualize a successful shot will achieve it 67% of the time, those that don't visualize will only achieve it 54% of the time.

In short, it works.

To visualize simply create a scene in your mind of what you want to happen in your game. Picture it over and over again in the build-up to the game. Your mind will start to believe the scene is real and that you can achieve what you're visualizing. You'll be surprised at how much difference it makes during your game!

Meditation

Meditation is more than just sitting calmly, it's an opportunity to focus your mind. You'll need to find a quiet space and get comfortable. It's generally recommended to sit somewhere with back support. Being comfortable ensures you can clear your mind and focus on one thing. It could be an element of your game or simply something going on in your life.

Focusing on one thing will help you put things into perspective, keeping your mind free of anxiety and encouraging a feeling of positivity. It also improves your ability to focus, which can be extremely beneficial during any sport.

You are also likely to find it easier to "dig deep" when the game is going against you. This is because you can recognize feelings of being overwhelmed and use your meditation techniques to calm yourself and regain focus.

Of course, it also helps you regulate your emotions and prevents you from playing in anger. Complement your meditation with controlled breathing exercises to increase your mental clarity and positive mindset.

Research

Research is often overlooked by players but it's essential if you want to win and, more importantly, feel capable of winning. You simply need to research your opponents and the game. The more you know about the game options and the way that opponents play, the easier it is to devise a winning strategy.

The reason is simple, when you understand how someone is likely to play and can devise a strategy to beat them, you'll instantly feel more confident going into the game. Confidence is a vital part of your positive mindset and believing that you can prevail.

Research also allows you to review your own game footage and identify what you are doing well and what you are struggling with. This will allow you to create targeted practice sessions designed to improve your performance and your confidence in your ability to win.

Listen to Criticism

Most people don't like to be criticized. It's like being told you're wrong and that generally stings. However, if you want to be the best at your sport, you need to learn to accept criticism, especially when it's from someone you trust.

Criticism can help you identify where you are going wrong, where you are underperforming, and which elements of your game are your weakest. It may be hard facing these facts but, listening to what others have to say and then working on these aspects will help you become a better player.

The act of listening, adapting, and improving will also help you to feel more positive. As we've established, a positive mindset is instrumental to success in your chosen sport. Just look at the legends in this book, none of them would have become legends unless they were positive that they could perform and win. That stems from believing in themselves first, something that you can also do.

Made in United States
Troutdale, OR
12/07/2024

26063080R00076